Live
Not by
Lies

Live
Not by
Lies

A MANUAL FOR
CHRISTIAN DISSIDENTS

ROD DREHER

SENTINEL

Sentinel
An imprint of Penguin Random House LLC
penguinrandomhouse.com

Most Sentinel books are available at a discount when purchased in quantity for sales
promotions or corporate use. Special editions, which include personalized covers, excerpts,
and corporate imprints, can be created when purchased in large quantities. For more
information, please call (212) 572-2232 or email specialmarkets@penguinrandomhouse.com.
Your local bookstore can also assist with discounted bulk purchases using the Penguin
Random House corporate Business-to-Business program. For assistance in locating a
participating retailer, email B2B@penguinrandomhouse.com.

Library of Congress Cataloging-in-Publication Data

Names: Dreher, Rod, author.
Title: Live not by lies : a manual for Christian dissidents / Rod Dreher.
Description: New York City : Sentinel, 2020. | Includes bibliographical
references and index.
Identifiers: LCCN 2020022423 (print) | LCCN 2020022424 (ebook) |
ISBN 9780593087398 (hardcover) | ISBN 9780593087404 (ebook)
Subjects: LCSH: Christians—Political activity. | Christianity and
politics—United States. | Liberalism—United States. | Truthfulness and
falsehood—United States. | Christianity and culture—United States.
Classification: LCC BR516 .D695 2020 (print) | LCC BR516 (ebook) |
DDC 277.308/3—dc23
LC record available at https://lccn.loc.gov/2020022423
LC ebook record available at https://lccn.loc.gov/2020022424

Printed in the United States of America
1   3   5   7   9   10   8   6   4   2

Book design by Cassandra Garruzzo

To the memory of
Father Tomislav Kolaković
(1906–1990)

CONTENTS

INTRODUCTION

There always is this fallacious belief: "It would not be the
same here; here such things are impossible." Alas, all the evil
of the twentieth century is possible everywhere on earth.

ALEKSANDR SOLZHENITSYN[1]

I n 1989, the Berlin Wall fell, and with it Soviet totalitarianism.
Gone was the communist police state that had enslaved Russia
and half of Europe. The Cold War that had dominated the second half of the twentieth century came to a close. Democracy and
capitalism bloomed in the formerly captive nations. The age of
totalitarianism passed into oblivion, never again to menace humanity.

Or so the story goes. I, along with most Americans, believed
that the menace of totalitarianism had passed. Then, in the spring
of 2015, I received a phone call from an anxious stranger.

The caller was an eminent American physician. He told me
that his elderly mother, a Czechoslovak immigrant to the United
States, had spent six years of her youth as a political prisoner in her
homeland. She had been part of the Catholic anti-communist

resistance. Now in her nineties and living with her son and his family, the old woman had recently told her American son that events in the United States today reminded her of when communism first came to Czechoslovakia.

What prompted her concern? News reports about the social-media mob frenzy against a small-town Indiana pizzeria whose Evangelical Christian owners told a reporter they would not cater a same-sex wedding. So overwhelming were the threats against their lives and property, including a user on the Twitter social media platform who tweeted a call for people to burn down the pizzeria, that the restaurant owners closed their doors for a time. Meanwhile, liberal elites, especially in the media, normally so watchful against the danger of mobs threatening the lives and livelihoods of minorities, were untroubled by the assault on the pizzeria, which occurred in the context of the broader debate about the clash between gay rights and religious liberty.

The US-born doctor said he had heard his immigrant parents warn him about the dangers of totalitarianism all his life. He hadn't worried—after all, this is America, the land of liberty, of individual rights, one nation under God and the rule of law. America was born out of a quest for religious liberty, and had always been proud of the First Amendment to the US Constitution that guaranteed it. But now there was something about what was happening in Indiana that made him think: *What if they were right?*

It's easy to laugh this kind of thing off. Many of us with aging parents are accustomed to having to talk them down from the ledge, so to speak, after a cable news program stoked their fear and anxiety about the world outside their front door. I assumed that this was probably the case with the elderly Czech woman.

But there was something about the tension in the doctor's voice, and the fact that he felt compelled to reach out to a journalist he didn't even know, telling me that it would be too dangerous for me to use his name if I wrote about him, that rattled me. His question became my question: *What if the old Czech woman sees something the rest of us do not?* What if we really are witnessing a turn toward totalitarianism in the Western liberal democracies, and can't see it because it takes a form different from the old kind?

During the next few years, I spoke with many men and women who had once lived under communism. I asked them what they thought of the old woman's declaration. Did they also think that life in America is drifting toward some sort of totalitarianism?

They all said *yes*—often emphatically. They were usually surprised by my question because they consider Americans to be hopelessly naive on the subject. In talking at length to some of the emigrants who found refuge in America, I discovered that they are genuinely angry that their fellow Americans don't recognize what is happening.

What makes the emerging situation in the West similar to what they fled? After all, every society has rules and taboos and mechanisms to enforce them. What unnerves those who lived under Soviet communism is this similarity: Elites and elite institutions are abandoning old-fashioned liberalism, based in defending the rights of the individual, and replacing it with a progressive creed that regards justice in terms of groups. It encourages people to identify with groups—ethnic, sexual, and otherwise—and to think of Good and Evil as a matter of power dynamics among the groups. A utopian vision drives these progressives, one that compels them to seek to rewrite history and reinvent language to reflect their ideals of social justice.

Further, these utopian progressives are constantly changing the standards of thought, speech, and behavior. You can never be sure when those in power will come after you as a villain for having said or done something that was perfectly fine the day before. And the consequences for violating the new taboos are extreme, including losing your livelihood and having your reputation ruined forever.

People are becoming instant pariahs for having expressed a politically incorrect opinion, or in some other way provoking a progressive mob, which amplifies its scapegoating through social and conventional media. Under the guise of "diversity," "inclusivity," "equity," and other egalitarian jargon, the Left creates powerful mechanisms for controlling thought and discourse and marginalizes dissenters as evil.

It is very hard for Americans who have never lived through this kind of ideological fog to recognize what is happening. To be sure, whatever this is, it is not a carbon copy of life in the Soviet Bloc nations, with their secret police, their gulags, their strict censorship, and their material deprivation. That is precisely the problem, these émigrés warn. The fact that relative to Soviet Bloc conditions, life in the West remains so free and so prosperous is what blinds Americans to the mounting threat to our liberty. That, and the way those who take away freedom couch it in the language of liberating victims from oppression.

"I was born and raised in the Soviet Union, and I'm frankly stunned by how similar some of these developments are to the way Soviet propaganda operated," says one professor, now living in the Midwest.

Another émigré professor, this one from Czechoslovakia, was equally blunt. He told me that he began noticing a shift a decade or so ago: friends would lower their voices and look over their shoulders when expressing conservative views. When he expressed his conservative beliefs in a normal tone of voice, the Americans would start to fidget and constantly scan the room to see who might be listening.

"I grew up like this," he tells me, "but it was not supposed to be happening here."

What *is* happening here? A progressive—and profoundly anti-Christian militancy—is steadily overtaking society; one described by Pope Benedict XVI as a "worldwide dictatorship of seemingly humanistic ideologies" that pushes dissenters to society's margins. Benedict called this a manifestation of "the spiritual power of the Antichrist."[2] This spiritual power takes material form in government and private institutions, in corporations, in academia and media, and in the changing practices of everyday American life. It is empowered by unprecedented technological capabilities to surveil private life. There is virtually nowhere left to hide.

The old, hard totalitarianism had a vision for the world that required the eradication of Christianity. The new, soft totalitarianism does too, and we are not equipped to resist its sneakier attack.

As we know, communism was militantly atheistic and declared religion to be its mortal enemy. The Soviets and their European allies murdered clergy and cast an uncounted number of believers, both ordained and lay, into prisons and work camps, where many suffered torture.

Today? The Western world has become post-Christian, with large numbers of those born after 1980 rejecting religious faith. This means that they will not only oppose Christians when we stand up for our principles—in particular, in defense of the traditional family, of male and female gender roles, and of the sanctity of human life—but also they will not even understand why they should tolerate dissent based in religious belief.

We cannot hope to resist the coming soft totalitarianism if we do not have our spiritual lives in order. This is the message of Aleksandr Solzhenitsyn, the great anti-communist dissident, Nobel laureate, and Orthodox Christian. He believed the core of the crisis that created and sustained communism was not political but spiritual.

After the publication of his *Gulag Archipelago* exposed the rottenness of Soviet totalitarianism and made Solzhenitsyn a global hero, Moscow finally expelled him to the West. On the eve of his forced exile, Solzhenitsyn published a final message to the Russian people, titled "Live Not by Lies!" In the essay, Solzhenitsyn challenged the claim that the totalitarian system was so powerful that the ordinary man and woman cannot change it.

Nonsense, he said. The foundation of totalitarianism is an ideology made of lies. The system depends for its existence on a people's fear of challenging the lies. Said the writer, "Our way must be: *Never knowingly support lies!*"[3] You may not have the strength to stand up in public and say what you really believe, but you can at least refuse to affirm what you do *not* believe. You may not be able to overthrow totalitarianism, but you can find within yourself and your community the means to live in the dignity of truth. If we must live under the dictatorship of lies, the writer said, then our response must be: "Let their rule hold *not through me!*"

What does it mean for us today to live not by lies? That is the question this book explores through interviews with and testaments left by Christians (and others) from throughout the Soviet Bloc who lived through totalitarianism, and who share the wisdom they gained through hard experience.

Part one of this book makes the case that despite its superficial permissiveness, liberal democracy is degenerating into something resembling the totalitarianism over which it triumphed in the Cold War. It explores the sources of totalitarianism, revealing the troubling parallels between contemporary society and the ones that gave birth to twentieth-century totalitarianism. It will also examine two particular factors that define the rising soft totalitarianism: the ideology of "social justice," which dominates academia and other major institutions, and surveillance technology, which has become ubiquitous not from government decree but through the persuasiveness of consumer capitalism. This section ends with a look at the key role intellectuals played in the Bolshevik Revolution and why we cannot afford to laugh off the ideological excesses of our own politically correct intelligentsia.

Part two examines in greater detail forms, methods, and sources of resistance to soft totalitarianism's lies. Why is religion and the hope it gives at the core of effective resistance? What does the willingness to suffer have to do with living in truth? Why is the family the most important cell of opposition? How does faithful fellowship provide resilience in the face of persecution? How can we learn to recognize totalitarianism's false messaging and fight its deceit?

How did these oppressed believers get through it? How did they protect themselves and their families? How did they keep their faith, their integrity, even their sanity? Why are they so anxious about the West's future? Are we capable of hearing them, or will we continue to rest easy in the delusion that it can't happen here?

A Soviet-born émigré who teaches in a university deep in the US heartland stresses the urgency of Americans taking people like her seriously.

"You will not be able to predict what will be held against you tomorrow," she warns. "You have no idea what completely normal thing you do today, or say today, will be used against you to destroy you. This is what people in the Soviet Union saw. We know how this works."

On the other hand, my Czech émigré friend advised me not to waste time writing this book.

"People will have to live through it first to understand," he says cynically. "Any time I try to explain current events and their meaning to my friends or acquaintances, I am met with blank stares or downright nonsense."

Maybe he is right. But for the sake of his children and mine, I wrote this book to prove him wrong.

PART ONE

Understanding Soft Totalitarianism

CHAPTER ONE

Kolaković the Prophet

S ometimes, a stranger who sees deeper and farther than the crowd appears to warn of trouble coming. These stories often end with people disbelieving the prophet and suffering for their blindness. Here, though, is a tale about a people who heard the prophet's warnings, did as he advised, and were ready when the crisis struck.

In 1943, a Jesuit priest and anti-fascist activist named Tomislav Poglajen fled his native Croatia one step ahead of the Gestapo and settled in Czechoslovakia. To conceal himself from the Nazis, he assumed his Slovak mother's name—Kolaković—and took up a teaching position in Bratislava, the capital of the Slovak region, which had become an independent vassal state of Hitler. The priest, thirty-seven years old and with a thick shock of prematurely white hair, had spent some his priestly training studying the Soviet Union. He believed that the defeat of Nazi totalitarianism would occasion a great conflict between Soviet totalitarianism and the liberal democratic West. Though Father Kolaković worried about the threats to Christian life and witness from the rich, materialistic West, he was far more concerned about the dangers of communism, which he correctly saw as an imperialistic ideology.

By the time Father Kolaković reached Bratislava, it was clear that the Red Army would defeat the Germans in the East. In fact, in 1944, the Czech government in exile—which also represented Slovaks who refused to accept the nominally independent Slovak state—made a formal agreement with Stalin, guaranteeing that after driving the Nazis out, the Soviets would give the reunited nation its freedom.

Because he knew how the Soviets thought, Father Kolaković knew this was a lie. He warned Slovak Catholics that when the war ended, Czechoslovakia would fall to the rule of a Soviet puppet government. He dedicated himself to preparing them for persecution.

The Unready Christians of Slovakia

Father Kolaković knew that the clericalism and passivity of traditional Slovak Catholicism would be no match for communism. For one thing, he correctly foresaw that the communists would try to control the Church by subduing the clergy. For another, he understood that the spiritual trials awaiting believers under communism would put them to an extreme test. The charismatic pastor preached that only a total life commitment to Christ would enable them to withstand the coming trial.

"Give yourself totally to Christ, throw all your worries and desires on him, for he has a wide back, and you will witness miracles," the priest said, in the recollection of one disciple.[1]

Giving oneself totally to Christ was not an abstraction or a pious thought. It needed to be concrete, and it needed to be communal. The total destruction of the First World War opened the eyes of younger Catholics to the need for a new evangelization. A Belgian priest named Joseph Cardijn, whose father had been killed in a mining accident, started a lay movement to do this among the working class. These were the Young Christian Workers, called "Jocists" after the initials of their name in French. Inspired by the Jocist example, Father Kolaković adapted it to the needs of the Catholic Church in German-occupied Slovakia. He established cells of faithful young Catholics who came together for prayer, study, and fellowship.

The refugee priest taught the young Slovak believers that every person must be accountable to God for his actions. Freedom is responsibility, he stressed; it is a means to live within the truth. The motto of the Jocists became the motto for what Father Kolaković called his "Family": "See. Judge. Act." *See* meant to be awake to realities around you. *Judge* was a command to discern soberly the meaning of those realities in light of what you know to be true, especially from the teachings of the Christian faith. After you reach a conclusion, then you are to *act* to resist evil.

Václav Vaško, a Kolaković follower, recalled late in his life that Father Kolaković's ministry excited so many young Catholics because it energized the laity and gave them a sense of leadership responsibility.

"It is remarkable how Kolaković almost instantly succeeded in creating a community of trust and mutual friendship from a diverse grouping of people (priests, religious and lay people of different ages, education, or spiritual maturity)," Vaško wrote.

The Family groups came together at first for Bible study and prayer, but soon began listening to Father Kolaković lecture on philosophy, sociology, and intellectual topics. Father Kolaković also trained his young followers in how to work secretly, and to withstand the interrogation that he said would surely come.

The Family expanded its small groups quickly across the nation. "By the end of the school year 1944," Vaško said, "it would have been difficult to find a faculty or secondary school in Bratislava or larger cities where our circles did not operate."

In 1946, Czech authorities deported the activist priest. Two years later, communists seized total power, just as Father Kolaković had predicted. Within several years, almost all of the Family had been imprisoned and the Czechoslovak institutional church brutalized into submission. But when the Family members emerged from prison in the 1960s, they began to do as their spiritual father had taught them. Father Kolaković's top two lieutenants—physician Silvester Krčméry and priest Vladimír Jukl—quietly set up Christian circles around the country and began to build the underground church.

The underground church, led by the visionary cleric's spiritual children and grandchildren, became the principle means of anti-communist dissent for the next forty years. It was they who organized a mass 1988 public demonstration in Bratislava, the Slovak capital, demanding religious liberty. The Candle Demonstration was the first major protest against the state. It kicked off the Velvet Revolution, which brought down the communist regime a year later. Though Slovak Christians were among the most persecuted in the Soviet Bloc, the Catholic Church there thrived in resistance because one man saw what was coming and prepared his people.

The New Totalitarianism

Why did Father Kolaković know what was coming to the people of Central Europe? He was not supernaturally gifted, at least not that we know. Rather, he had studied Soviet communism intensely to prepare for missionary work in Russia and understood how the Soviets thought and behaved. He could read the geopolitical signs of the times. And as a priest who had been organizing Catholic resistance to the Nazi version of totalitarianism, he had on-the-ground experience with clandestine combat against monstrous ideology.

Today's survivors of Soviet communism are, in their way, our own Kolakovićes, warning us of a coming totalitarianism—a form of government that combines political authoritarianism with an ideology that seeks to control all aspects of life. This totalitarianism won't look like the USSR's. It's not establishing itself through "hard" means like armed revolution, or enforcing itself with gulags. Rather, it exercises control, at least initially, in soft forms. This totalitarianism is therapeutic. It masks its hatred of dissenters from its utopian ideology in the guise of helping and healing.

To grasp the threat of totalitarianism, it's important to understand the difference between it and simple authoritarianism. Authoritarianism is what you have when the state monopolizes political control. That is mere dictatorship—bad, certainly, but totalitarianism is much worse. According to Hannah Arendt, the foremost scholar of totalitarianism, a totalitarian society is one in which an ideology seeks to displace all prior traditions and institutions, with the goal of bringing all aspects of society under control of that ideology. A totalitarian state is one that aspires to nothing less than defining and controlling reality. Truth is whatever the rulers decide it is. As Arendt has written, wherever totalitarianism has ruled, "[I]t has begun to destroy the essence of man."[2]

As part of its quest to define reality, a totalitarian state seeks not just to control your actions but also your thoughts and emotions. The ideal subject of a totalitarian state is someone who has learned to love Big Brother.

Back in the Soviet era, totalitarianism demanded love for the Party, and compliance with the Party's demands was enforced by the state. Today's totalitarianism demands allegiance to a set of progressive beliefs, many of which are incompatible with logic—and certainly with Christianity. Compliance is forced less by the state than by elites who form public opinion, and by private corporations that, thanks to technology, control our lives far more than we would like to admit.

Many conservatives today fail to grasp the gravity of this threat, dismissing it as mere "political correctness"—a previous generation's disparaging term for so-called "wokeness." It's easy to dismiss people like the former Soviet professor as hysterical if you think of what's happening today as nothing more than the return of the left-wing campus kookiness of the 1990s. Back then, the standard conservative response was dismissive. *Wait till those kids get out into the real world and have to find a job.*

Well, they did—and they brought the campus to corporate America, to the legal and medical professions, to media, to elementary and secondary schools, and to other institutions of American life. In this cultural revolution, which intensified in the spring and summer of 2020, they are attempting to turn the entire country into a "woke" college campus.

Today in our societies, dissenters from the woke party line find their businesses, careers, and reputations destroyed. They are pushed out of the public square, stigmatized, canceled, and demonized as racists, sexists, homophobes, and the like. And they are afraid to resist, because they are confident that no one will join them or defend them.

The Gentleness of Soft Totalitarianism

It's possible to miss the onslaught of totalitarianism, precisely because we have a misunderstanding of how its power works. In 1951, poet and literary critic Czesław Miłosz, exiled to the West from his native Poland as an anti-communist dissident, wrote that Western people misunderstand the nature of communism because they think of it only in terms of "might and coercion."

"That is wrong," he wrote. "There is an internal longing for harmony and happiness that lies deeper than ordinary fear or the desire to escape misery or physical destruction."[3]

In *The Captive Mind*, Miłosz said that communist ideology filled a void that had opened in the lives of early-twentieth-century intellectuals, most of whom had ceased to believe in religion.

Today's left-wing totalitarianism once again appeals to an internal hunger, specifically the hunger for a just society, one that vindicates and liberates the historical victims of oppression. It masquerades as kindness, demonizing dissenters and disfavored demographic groups to protect the feelings of "victims" in order to bring about "social justice."

The contemporary cult of social justice identifies members of certain social groups as victimizers, as scapegoats, and calls for their suppression as a matter of righteousness. In this way, the so-called social justice warriors (aka SJWs), who started out as liberals animated by an urgent compassion, end by abandoning authentic liberalism and embracing an aggressive and punitive politics that resembles Bolshevism, as the Soviet style of communism was first called.

At the turn of the twenty-first century, the cultural critic René Girard prophetically warned: "The current process of spiritual demagoguery and rhetorical overkill has transformed the concern for victims into a totalitarian command and a permanent inquisition."[4]

This is what the survivors of communism are saying to us: liberalism's admirable care for the weak and marginalized is fast turning into a monstrous ideology that, if it is not stopped, will transform liberal democracy into a softer, therapeutic form of totalitarianism.

The Therapeutic as the
Postmodern Mode of Existence

Soft totalitarianism exploits decadent modern man's preference for personal pleasure over principles, including political liberties. The public will support, or at least not oppose, the coming soft totalitarianism, not because it fears the imposition of cruel punishments but because it will be more or less satisfied by hedonistic comforts. *Nineteen Eighty-Four* is not the novel that previews what's coming; it's rather Aldous Huxley's *Brave New World*. The contemporary social critic James Poulos calls this the "Pink Police State": an informal arrangement in which people will surrender political rights in exchange for guarantees of personal pleasure.

Soft totalitarianism, as we will see in a later chapter, makes use of advanced surveillance technology not (yet) imposed by the state, but rather welcomed by consumers as aids to lifestyle convenience—and in the postpandemic environment, likely needed for public health. It is hard to get worked up over Big Brother when you have already grown accustomed to Big Data closely monitoring your private life via apps, credit cards, and smart devices, which make life so much easier and more pleasurable. In Orwell's fictional dystopia, the state installed "telescreens" in private homes to keep track of individual's lives. Today we install smart speakers into our homes to increase our sense of well-being.

How did maximizing a feeling of well-being become the ultimate goal of modern people and societies? The American sociologist and cultural critic Philip Rieff was not a religious believer, but few prophets have written more piercingly about the nature of the cultural revolution that overtook the West in the twentieth century that defines the core of soft totalitarianism.

In his landmark 1966 book, *The Triumph of the Therapeutic*, Rieff said the death of God in the West had given birth to a new civilization devoted to liberating the individual to seek his own pleasures and to managing emergent anxieties. Religious Man, who lived according to belief in transcendent principles that ordered human life around communal purposes, had given way to Psychological Man, who believed that there was no transcendent order and that life's purpose was to find one's own way experimentally. Man no longer understood himself to be a pilgrim on a meaningful journey with others, but as a tourist who traveled through life according to his own self-designed itinerary, with personal happiness his ultimate goal.

This was a revolution even more radical than the 1917 Bolshevik event, said Rieff. For the first time, humankind was seeking to create a civilization based on the negation of any binding transcendent order. The Bolsheviks may have been godless, but even they believed that there was a metaphysical order, one that demanded that individuals subordinate their personal desires to a higher cause. Almost a quarter century before the fall of the Berlin Wall, Rieff predicted that communism would not be able to withstand the cultural revolution coming from the West, one that purported to set the individual free to pursue hedonism and individualism. If there is no sacred order, then the original promise of the serpent in the Garden of Eden—"[Y]e shall be as gods"—is the foundational principle of the new culture.

Rieff saw, however, that you could not have culture without cult—that is, without shared belief in and submission to a sacred order, what you get is an "anti-culture." An anti-culture is inherently unstable, said Rieff, but he doubted that people brought up in this social order would ever be willing to return to the old ways.

Even church leaders, he wrote, were lying to themselves about the ability of the institutions they led to resist the therapeutic. Rieff foresaw the future of religion as devolution into watery spirituality, which could accommodate anything. Rieff lived long enough to see his 1966 prediction come true. In 2005, the sociologists of religion Christian Smith and Melinda Lundquist Denton coined the phrase Moralistic Therapeutic Deism to describe the decadent form that Christianity (and all faiths, in fact) had taken in contemporary America. It consisted of the general belief that God exists, and wants nothing more from us than to be nice and to be happy.

In therapeutic culture, which has everywhere triumphed, the great sin is to stand in the way of the freedom of others to find happiness as they wish. This goes hand in hand with the sexual revolution, which, along with ethnic and gender identity politics, replaced the failed economic class struggle as the utopian focus of the post-1960s radical left. These cultural revolutionaries found an ally in advanced capitalism, which teaches that nothing should exist outside of the market mechanism and its sorting of value according to human desires.

The Cold War and the fallout from cultural conflicts of the sixties and seventies drove many white conservative Christians to identify with the Republican Party and free-market economics as consonant with Christian morality. Relativism clad in free-market dogma aided the absorption of the therapeutic ethos by the Religious Right. After all, if true freedom is defined as freedom of choice, as opposed to the classical concept of choosing virtue, then the door is wide open to reforming religion along therapeutic lines centered around subjective experience. This is why so many conservative Christians did not see, and still cannot explain, the ongoing victories of transgenderism in the culture war. The transgender phenomenon, which requires affirming psychology over biological reality, is a logical culmination of a process that started centuries earlier.

Christian resistance on a large scale to the anti-culture has been fruitless, and is likely to be for the foreseeable future. Why? Because the spirit of the therapeutic has conquered the churches as well—even those populated by Christians who identify as conservative. Relatively few contemporary Christians are prepared to suffer for the faith, because the therapeutic society that has formed them denies the purpose of suffering in the first place, and the idea of bearing pain for the sake of truth seems ridiculous.

13

Ketman and the Pill of Murti-Bing

It is difficult for people raised in the free world to grasp the breadth and the depth of lying required simply to exist under communism. All the lies, and lies about lies, that formed the communist order were built on the basis of this foundational lie: the communist state is the sole source of truth. Orwell said in *Nineteen Eighty-Four*: "The Party told you to reject the evidence of your eyes and ears. It was their final, most essential command."[5]

Under the dictatorship of Big Brother, the Party understands that by changing language—*Newspeak* is the Party's word for the jargon it imposes on society—it controls the categories in which people think. "Freedom" is slavery, "truth" is falsehood, and so forth. *Doublethink*—"holding two contradictory beliefs in one's mind simultaneously, and accepting both of them"—is how people learn to submit their minds to the Party's ideology. If the Party says $2 + 2 = 5$, then $2 + 2 = 5$. The goal is to convince the person that all truth exists within the mind, and the rightly ordered mind believes whatever the Party says is true.

Orwell writes:

> It was as though some huge force were pressing down upon you—something that penetrated inside your skull, battering against your brain, frightening you out of your beliefs, persuading you, almost, to deny the evidence of your senses. In the end the Party would announce that two and two made five, and you would have to believe it. It was inevitable that they should make that claim sooner or later:

the logic of their position demanded it. Not merely the validity of experience but the very existence of external reality was tacitly denied by their philosophy. The heresy of heresies was common sense.[6]

In our time, we do not have an all-powerful state forcing this on us. This dictatorship is far more subtle. Under soft totalitarianism, the media, academia, corporate America, and other institutions are practicing Newspeak and compelling the rest of us to engage in doublethink every day. *Men have periods. The woman standing in front of you is to be called "he." Diversity and inclusion means excluding those who object to ideological uniformity. Equity means treating persons unequally, regardless of their skills and achievements, to achieve an ideologically correct result.*

To update an Orwell line to our own situation: "The Office of Diversity, Equity, and Inclusion told you to reject the evidence of your eyes and ears. It was their final, most essential command."

Many Christians will see through these lies today but will choose not to speak up. Their silence will not save them and will instead corrode them, according to Miłosz.

In his writing about communism's insidiousness, Miłosz referenced a 1932 novel, *Insatiability*. In it, Polish writer Stanisław Witkiewicz wrote of a near-future dystopia in which the people were culturally exhausted and had fallen into decadence. A Mongol army from the East threatened to overrun them.

As part of the plan to take over the nation, people began turning up in the streets selling "the pill of Murti-Bing," named after a Mongolian philosopher who found a way to embody his "don't worry, be happy" philosophy in a tablet. Those who took the Pill of Murti-Bing quit worrying about life, even though things were falling apart around them. When the Eastern army arrived, it surrendered happily, its soldiers relieved to have found deliverance from their internal tension and struggles.

Only the peace didn't last. "But since they could not rid themselves completely of their former personalities," writes Miłosz, "they became schizophrenics."[7]

What do you do when the Pill of Murti-Bing stops working and you find yourself living under a dictatorship of official lies in which anyone who contradicts the party line goes to jail?

You become an actor, says Miłosz. You learn the practice of *ketman*. This is the Persian word for the practice of maintaining an outward appearance of Islamic orthodoxy while inwardly dissenting. *Ketman* was the strategy everyone who wasn't a true believer in communism had to adopt to stay out of trouble. It is a form of mental self-defense.

What is the difference between *ketman* and plain old hypocrisy? As Miłosz explains, having to be "on" all the time inevitably changes a person. An actor who inhabits his role around the clock eventually becomes the character he plays. *Ketman* is worse than hypocrisy, because living by it all the time corrupts your character and ultimately everything in society.

Miłosz identified eight different types of *ketman* under communism. For example, "professional *ketman*" is when you convince yourself that it's okay to live a lie in the workplace, because that's what you have to do to have the freedom to do good work. "Metaphysical *ketman*" is the deepest form of the strategy, a defense against "total degradation." It consists of convincing yourself that it really is possible for you to be a loyal opponent of the new regime while working with it. Christians who collaborated with communist regimes were guilty of metaphysical *ketman*. In fact, says Miłosz, it represents the ultimate victory of the Big Lie over the individual's soul.

Under the emerging tyranny of wokeness, conservatives, including conservative Christians, learn to practice one or more forms of *ketman*. The ones who are most deeply deceived are those who convince themselves that they can live honestly within woke systems by outwardly conforming and learning how to adapt their convictions to the new order. Miłosz had their number: "They swindle the devil who thinks he is swindling them. But the devil knows what they think and is satisfied."[8]

Living in Truth

On the day of his Moscow arrest—February 12, 1974—Aleksandr Solzhenitsyn published what would be his final message to the Russian people before the government exiled him to the West. In the title of the exhortation, he urged the Russian people to "live not by lies!"[9]

What did it mean to live by lies? It meant, Solzhenitsyn writes, accepting without protest all the falsehoods and propaganda that the state compelled its citizens to affirm—or at least not to oppose—to get along peaceably under totalitarianism. Everybody says that they have no choice but to conform, says Solzhenitsyn, and to accept powerlessness. But that is the lie that gives all the other lies their malign force. The ordinary man may not be able to overturn the kingdom of lies, but he can at least say that he is not going to be its loyal subject.

"We are not called upon to step out onto the square and shout out the truth, to say out loud what we think—this is scary, we are not ready," he writes. "But let us at least refuse to say what we *do not* think!"

For example, says Solzhenitsyn, a man who refuses to live by lies:

- Will not say, write, affirm, or distribute anything that distorts the truth
- Will not go to a demonstration or participate in a collective action unless he truly believes in the cause
- Will not take part in a meeting in which the discussion is forced and no one can speak the truth
- Will not vote for a candidate or proposal he considers to be "dubious or unworthy"
- Will walk out of an event "as soon as he hears the speaker utter a lie, ideological drivel, or shameless propaganda"
- Will not support journalism that "distorts or hides the underlying facts"

"This is by no means an exhaustive list of the possible and necessary ways of evading lies," Solzhenitsyn writes. "But he who begins to cleanse himself will, with a cleansed eye, easily discern yet other opportunities."[10]

The task of the Christian dissident today is to personally commit herself to live not by lies. How can she do that alone? She needs to draw close to authentic spiritual leadership—clerical, lay, or both—and form small cells of fellow believers with whom she can pray, sing, study Scripture, and read other books important to their mission. With her cell, the dissident discusses the issues and challenges facing them as Christians, especially challenges to their liberties. They employ the Kolaković method of See, Judge, Act. That is, identify the challenge, discern together its meaning, then act on your conclusions.

In the long term, today's Christian dissidents must come to think of themselves as heirs to Father Kolaković's Family, spreading the movement throughout the country and helping sympathetic believers prepare for days of suffering and resistance ahead. Soft totalitarianism is coming. As we will see in the next chapter, the groundwork has already been laid.

CHAPTER TWO

Our Pre-Totalitarian Culture

All the young are candidates for the solutions of
communism or fascism when there are no alternatives
to despair or dissipation.

NADINE GORDIMER[1]

A t dinner in a Russian Orthodox family's apartment in the
Moscow suburbs, I was shaken by our table talk of Soviet
oppression through which the father and mother of the
household had lived. "I don't understand how anybody could
have believed what the Bolsheviks promised," I said glibly.

"You don't understand it?" said the father at the head of the
table. "Let me explain it to you." He then launched into a three-
hundred-year historical review that ended with the 1917 Revolution.

It was a pitiless tale of rich and powerful elites, including church bureaucrats, treating peasants little better than animals.

"The Bolsheviks were evil," the father said. "But you can see where they came from."

The Russian man was right. I was chastened. The cruelty, the injustice, the implacability, and at times the sheer stupidity of the imperial Russian government and social order in no way justifies all that followed—but it does explain why the revolutionary Russian generation was so eager to place its hope in communism. It promised a road out of the muck and misery that had been the lot of the victimized Russian peasant since time out of mind.

The history of Russia on the verge of left-wing revolution is more relevant to contemporary America than most of us realize.

The Russia in which communism appeared had become a world power under the reign of the Romanov dynasty, but as the empire limped toward the twentieth century, it was falling apart. Though its rivals were fast industrializing, Russia's agricultural economy and its peasantry remained mired in backwardness. A severe famine in 1891 shook the nation to the core and revealed the weakness of the tsarist system, which failed miserably to respond to the crisis. A young monarch, Nicholas II, came to power in 1894, but he proved incapable of meeting the agonizing challenges facing his government.

Past attempts to radicalize the peasantry went nowhere in the face of its profound conservatism. But by century's end, industrialization had created a large urban underclass of laborers who were cut off from their villages and thus from the traditions and religious beliefs that bound them. The laborers dwelled in misery in the cities, exploited by factory owners and unrelieved by the tsar. Calls for reform of the imperial structure—including the ossified Russian Orthodox Church—went ignored.

Few in Russian society, outside of the imperial court's bubble, believed that the system could carry on. But Tsar Nicholas II and his closest advisers insisted that sticking to the proven ways of traditional autocracy would get them through the crisis. The leadership of the church also ignored internal calls for reform from priests who could see the church's influence wasting away. Russia's intellectual and creative classes fell under the sway of Prometheanism, the belief that man has unlimited godlike powers to make the world to suit his desires.

In retrospect, this seems almost unbelievable. How could the Russians have been so blind? It was, in a sense, a problem of the imagination. Reflecting on the speed with which utopian dreams turned into a grisly nightmare, Solzhenitsyn observed:

If the intellectuals in the plays of Chekhov who spent all their time guessing what would happen in twenty, thirty, or forty years had been told that in forty years interrogation by torture would be practiced in Russia; that prisoners would have their skulls squeezed within iron rings; that a human being would be lowered into an acid bath; that they would be trussed up naked to be bitten by ants and bedbugs; that a ramrod heated over a primus stove would be thrust up their anal canal (the "secret brand"); that a man's genitals would be slowly crushed beneath the toe of a jackboot; and that, in the luckiest possible circumstances, prisoners would be tortured by being kept from sleeping for a week, by thirst, and by being beaten to a bloody pulp, not one of Chekhov's plays would have gotten to its end because all the heroes would have gone off to insane asylums.[2]

It wasn't just the tsarists who didn't see it coming but also the country's leading liberal minds. It was simply beyond their ability to conceive.

Why Communism Appealed to Russians

Marxism is a highly theoretical, abstract set of doctrines that cannot be easily grasped by nonspecialists. It took Russian intellectuals by storm because its evangelists presented Marxism as a secular religion for the post-religious age.

Though Karl Marx, communism's German-born prophet, despised religion, he gave birth to a vision of political economy that uncannily paralleled the promises of apocalyptic Christianity. The political philosophy that would come to bear his name construed history as the story of the struggle between classes. Marx believed that class inequality—caused by the rich exploiting the toiling masses—was responsible for the world's misfortune. Religion was, in Marx's words, "the opium of the people," functioning as a kind of drug that dulled their suffering and prevented them from seeing their true condition. Marx preached a revolution that would wrest control from the rich (capitalists) in the name of the proletariat (workers) and establish an all-powerful government that would redistribute resources justly before withering away. Crucially, Marx and his followers forecast the revolution as a bloody showdown between Good (the workers) and Evil (the capitalists) and prophesied the victory of justice and the establishment of an earthly paradise.

Marx believed that his teachings were based in science, which, in the nineteenth century, had displaced religion as the most important source of authority among intellectuals. The nineteenth century was the golden age of European liberalism, in which nations that had been ruled by kings and aristocracies struggled to reform themselves along constitutional, republican lines. Russia firmly rejected reform. Russian liberalism foundered in the face of tsarist autocracy and the indifference of the peasant masses.

As the century wore on, educated Russians were aware of how far their agrarian country was falling behind modernizing, industrializing Europe, both politically and economically. Younger Russians also keenly felt the shame of their liberal fathers' failures to change the system. In the midst of Russia's decline, Marxism appealed to restless young intellectuals who were sick of the old order, had lost faith in reforming it, and were desperate to tear the system down and replace it with something entirely different.

Marxism stood for the future. Marxism stood for progress. The gospel of Marxism lit a fire in the minds of prerevolutionary Russian radicals. Their priests and the prophets were their intellectuals, who were "religious about being secular." Writes historian Yuri Slezkine: "A conversion to socialism was a conversion to the intelligentsia, to a fusion of millenarian faith and lifelong learning."[3]

Far-left radicalism was initially spread among the intellectuals primarily through reading groups. Once you adopted the Marxist faith, everything else in life became illuminated. The intellectuals went into the world to preach this pseudoreligion to the workers. These missionaries, says Slezkine, made what religious believers would call prophetic revelations, and by appealing to hatred in their listeners' hearts, called them to conversion.

Once they had captured Russia's universities, the radicals took their gospel to the factories. Few of the workers were capable of understanding Marxist doctrine, but the missionaries taught it to those capable of translating the essentials into a form that ordinary people could grasp. These proselytizers spoke to the suffering of the people, to their sense of justice, to their often-justified resentment of their exploiters. The great famine of 1891–92 had laid bare the incompetence of the Russian ruling classes. The evangelists of Marxism issued forth prophetic revelations about the land of milk and honey awaiting the masses after the revolution swept away the ruling mandarins.

Most of the revolutionaries came from the privileged classes. Their parents ought to have known that this new political faith their children preached would, if realized, mean the collapse of the social order. Still, they would not reject their children. Writes Slezkine, "The 'students' were almost always abetted at home while still in school and almost never damned when they became revolutionaries."[4] Perhaps the mothers and fathers didn't want to alienate their sons and daughters. Perhaps they too, after the experience of the terrible famine and the incompetent state's inability to care for the starving, had lost faith in the system.

In 1905, waves of civil unrest swept across Russia. The empire's defeat in a war with Japan the year before further destabilized the throne and fostered discontent within the military. Widespread poverty and economic instability stirred up both the peasantry and industrial workers, who were finally listening to the radical student intellectuals. The "nationality problem"—the state's inability to deal fairly with the many non-Russian minorities living under imperial government—raised internal conflict to a fevered pitch. Nicholas II initially responded with characteristic repression, but the scale of the anti-state violence soon compelled him to agree to certain liberal reforms, including the creation of a weak parliament.

The 1905 Revolution bought the Romanov dynasty time, but Russian monarchy's doom was sealed with the arrival of the Great War in 1914. Russia's humiliating defeat called down the long-prophesied apocalypse in the form of the 1917 October Revolution led by Vladimir Lenin and his Bolshevik party. Among revolutionary Russia's far-left factions, Bolsheviks were relatively small in number, but under Lenin's forceful leadership, they were smart, ruthless, and determined. Their victory proved that under certain conditions, a clever, dedicated minority can gain absolute power over a disorganized, leaderless, and indifferent mass.

One year after the proletarian revolution, the Bolsheviks introduced mass ideological killing, calling it the Red Terror. Thus did the radical intelligentsia, with a mustard seed of faith, move the mountain that was Russia and hurl it into a sea of blood.

It was not supposed to happen there either. Even doctrinaire European Marxists believed there was no way agrarian Russia was ready for communist revolution. But it was.

Evangelizing Russia's Neighbors

It is true that communism came to Central Europe at the point of Soviet bayonets, but it is not the whole truth. World War I dramatically weakened civil society in those nations too, and inspired young intellectuals to embrace Marxism.

"In the 1930s, before the rise of the communist regime, there were already strong forces in the culture that paved the way for it," says Patrik Benda, a Prague political consultant, of his native Czechoslovakia. "All the artists and intellectuals advocated communist ideas, and if you didn't agree, you were marked for exclusion. This was almost two decades before actual communism took power."

The even worse catastrophe of World War II strengthened the case for communism. Having endured the agonies of Nazi occupation, many Central Europeans were desperate to believe in something that would guarantee them a bright future. One Czech survivor of the Nazi death camps later wrote that she joined the Communist Party because she mistakenly assumed that it was the polar opposite of Nazism.

When local communists seized power, backed by Soviet might, there was not much left within the exhausted populations with which to resist. Writes historian Anne Applebaum, "And so, the vast majority of Eastern Europeans did not make a pact with the devil or sell their soul to become informers but rather succumbed to the constant, all-encompassing, everyday psychological and economic pressure."[5]

This is how the peoples of Eastern Europe all fell under communist dictatorships propped up by Soviet power. For the people of those captive nations, totalitarianism meant the near-total destruction of any institutions independent of the state. It meant complete economic submission to the state and general material immiseration. It meant the politicization of all aspects of life, enforced by secret police, prisons, and labor camps. It meant the harsh persecution of religious believers, the crushing of free speech and expression, and the erasure of historical and cultural memory. And when some brave peoples—Hungarians in 1956, Czechs in 1968—stood up to their oppressors, Soviet and allied armed forces invaded to remind them who was the master and who were the slaves.

For over four decades, until communism's collapse in 1989, millions of Eastern Europeans endured this police-state captivity. For the Russian people, their enslavement to communism lasted decades longer, and was even harsher. True, communists in power held on to it through sheer terror and exercising a monopoly on force. But we cannot lose sight of the fact that communism didn't come from nowhere—that there really were people whose lives were so hard and hopeless that the utopian proclamations of Marxist zealots sounded something like salvation.

Under the right conditions, yes, it can happen here. It wouldn't happen in the same way as in Russia and Eastern Europe—times have changed—but the totalitarian temptation presents itself with a twenty-first-century face. The parallels between a declining United States and prerevolutionary Russia are not exact, but they are unnervingly close.

The old world of classical liberalism is dying throughout the Western world, but its successor has not yet been born. Economic stagnation, indebtedness, and widening gaps between the rich and everyone else are moving to the forefront of politics—and parties are moving toward ideological extremes. This pattern is replicating itself throughout Europe as centrist parties of left and right lose voters to more radicals in the Marxist tradition, or to right-wing populists.

Aside from shared social, institutional, and economic signs of decline, to which American elites seem blind and impotent to address, the US federal government's failure to respond effectively to the Covid-19 pandemic rhymed appallingly with the tsarist regime's embarrassing response to the famine of the 1890s. Both natural disasters caused mass suffering and revealed systemic decay in the habits and institutions of governing authority.

Unlike the imperial Russians, we are not likely to face widespread rioting and armed insurrection. There are no Lenins in exile, waiting to return in a sealed train to America to take command of the revolution. Relatively few people could be persuaded that Karl Marx has the answer to our problems. As far as we can tell, there is no new political religion brewing in beer halls or coffeehouses.

But that doesn't mean we aren't ripe for a new and different form of totalitarianism. The term *totalitarianism* was first used by supporters of fascist dictator Benito Mussolini, who defined totalitarianism concisely: "Everything within the state, nothing outside the state, nothing against the state." That is to say, totalitarianism is a state in which nothing can be permitted to exist that contradicts a society's ruling ideology.

What kind of people would be so demoralized that this— submission to a totalizing ideological program—sounds appealing? For the answer, we turn to, Hannah Arendt.

How to See Totalitarianism Coming

In 1951 after the end of World War II, Arendt published *The Origins of Totalitarianism*, the political philosopher's classic study of what had happened in Germany and the Soviet Union, in an attempt to understand how such radical ideologies had seized the minds of men.

According to Arendt, the following conditions tilled the ground, readying it for poisonous ideas planted by ideological activists.

LONELINESS AND SOCIAL ATOMIZATION

Totalitarian movements, said Arendt, are "mass organizations of atomized, isolated individuals." She continues:

> What prepares men for totalitarian domination in the non-totalitarian world, is the fact that loneliness, once a border-line experience usually suffered in certain marginal social conditions like old age, has become an everyday experience of the ever-growing masses of our century.[6]

The political theorist wrote those words in the 1950s, a period we look back on as a golden age of community cohesion. Today, loneliness is widely recognized by scientists as a critical social and even medical problem. In the year 2000, Harvard political scientist Robert Putnam published *Bowling Alone*, an acclaimed study documenting the steep decline of civil society since midcentury and the resulting atomization of America.

Since Putnam's book, we have experienced the rise of social media networks offering a facsimile of "connection." Yet we grow ever lonelier and more isolated. It is no coincidence that millennials and members of Generation Z register much higher rates of loneliness than older Americans, as well as significantly greater support for socialism. It's as if they aspire to a politics that can replace the community they wish they had.

Sooner or later, loneliness and isolation are bound to have political effects. The masses supporting totalitarian movements, says
Arendt, grew "out of the fragments of a highly atomized society
whose competitive structure and concomitant loneliness of the individual had been held in check only through membership in a
class."[7]

Civic trust is another bond that holds society together. Arendt
writes that the Soviet government, in an effort to monopolize control, caused the Russian people to turn on one another. In the
United States, we have seen nothing like the state aggressively dis-
mantling civil society—but it's happening all the same.

In *Bowling Alone*, Putnam documented the unraveling of civic
bonds since the 1950s. Americans attend fewer club meetings, have
fewer dinner parties, eat dinner together as a family less, and are
much less connected to their neighbors. They are disconnected
from political parties and more skeptical of institutions. They
spend much more time alone watching television or cocooning on
the internet. The result is that ordinary people feel more anxious,
isolated, and vulnerable.

A polity filled with alienated individuals who share little sense
of community and purpose are prime targets for totalitarian ideologies and leaders who promise solidarity and meaning.

LOSING FAITH IN HIERARCHIES AND INSTITUTIONS

Americans' loss of faith in institutions and hierarchies began in the
1960s. In Europe, though, it started in the immediate aftermath of
World War I. Surveying the political scene in Germany during the

1920s, Arendt noted a "terrifying negative solidarity" among people from diverse classes, united in their belief that all political parties were populated by fools.

Are we today really so different? According to Gallup, Americans' confidence in their institutions—political, media, religious, legal, medical, corporate—is at historic lows across the board. Only the military, the police, and small businesses retain the strong confidence of over 50 percent. Democratic norms are under strain in many industrialized nations, with the support for mainstream parties of left and right in decline.

In Europe of the 1920s, says Arendt, the first indication of the coming totalitarianism was the failure of established parties to attract younger members, and the willingness of the passive masses to consider radical alternatives to discredited establishment parties.

A loss of faith in democratic politics is a sign of a deeper and broader instability. As radical individualism has become more pervasive in our consumerist-driven culture, people have ceased to look outside themselves for authoritative sources of meaning. This is the fulfillment of modern liberalism's goal: to free the individual from any unchosen obligations.

But this imposes a terrible psychological burden on the individual, many of whom may seek deliverance in the certainties and solidarity offered by totalitarian movements.

Sociologist Émile Durkheim observed that many people who had been set free from the bonds of religion did not thrive in their liberty. In fact, they lost a shared sense of purpose, of meaning, and of community. A number of these despairing people committed suicide. According to Durkheim, what happened to individuals could also happen to societies.

You can destroy as much by failing to build as by actively wrecking. Philip Rieff said the collapse of a civilizational order begins when its elites cease to be able to transmit faith in its institutions and customs to younger generations. Political scientist Yascha Mounk, observing the collapse of liberal democratic values among American elites, tweeted:

> It's telling that, in the year of 2019, the notion that one purpose of civics education might be to convince students that there is in fact something worthwhile in our political system seems to strike many members of elite institutions as faintly bizarre.[8]

THE DESIRE TO TRANSGRESS AND DESTROY

The post-World War I generation of writers and artists were marked by their embrace and celebration of anti-cultural philosophies and acts as a way of demonstrating contempt for established hierarchies, institutions, and ways of thinking. Arendt said of some writers who glorified the will to power, "They read not Darwin but the Marquis de Sade."[9]

Her point was that these authors did not avail themselves of respectable intellectual theories to justify their transgressiveness. They immersed themselves in what is basest in human nature and regarded doing so as acts of liberation. Arendt's judgment of the postwar elites who recklessly thumbed their noses at respectability could easily apply to those of our own day who shove aside liberal principles like fair play, race neutrality, free speech, and free association as obstacles to equality. Arendt wrote:

The members of the elite did not object at all to paying a price, the destruction of civilization, for the fun of seeing how those who had been excluded unjustly in the past forced their way into it.[10]

Regarding transgressive sexuality as a social good was not an innovation of the sexual revolution. Like the contemporary West, late imperial Russia was also awash in what historian James Billington called "a preoccupation with sex that is quite without parallel in earlier Russian culture."[11] Among the social and intellectual elite, sexual adventurism, celebrations of perversion, and all manner of sensuality was common. And not just among the elites: the laboring masses, alone in the city, with no church to bind their consciences with guilt, or village gossips to shame them, found comfort in sex.

The end of official censorship after the 1905 uprising opened the floodgates to erotic literature, which found renewal in sexual passion. "The sensualism of the age was in a very intimate sense demonic,"[12] Billington writes, detailing how the figure of Satan became a Romantic hero for artists and musicians. They admired the diabolic willingness to stop at nothing to satisfy one's desires and to exercise one's will.

PROPAGANDA AND THE WILLINGNESS TO BELIEVE USEFUL LIES

Heda Margolius Kovály, a disillusioned Czech communist whose husband was executed after a 1952 show trial, reflects on the willingness of people to turn their backs on the truth for the sake of an ideological cause.

LIVE NOT BY LIES

It is not hard for a totalitarian regime to keep people ignorant. Once you relinquish your freedom for the sake of
"understood necessity," for Party discipline, for conformity
with the regime, for the greatness and glory of the Fatherland, or for any of the substitutes that are so convincingly
offered, you cede your claim to the truth. Slowly, drop by
drop, your life begins to ooze away just as surely as if you
had slashed your wrists; you have voluntarily condemned
yourself to helplessness.[13]

You can surrender your moral responsibility to be honest out of
misplaced idealism. You can also surrender it by hating others
more than you love truth. In pre-totalitarian states, Arendt writes,
hating "respectable society" was so narcotic that elites were willing to accept "monstrous forgeries in historiography" for the sake
of striking back at those who, in their view, had "excluded the
underprivileged and oppressed from the memory of mankind."[14]
For example, many who didn't really accept Marx's revisionist take
on history—that it is a manifestation of class struggle—were willing to affirm it because it was a useful tool to punish those they
despised.

Here's an important example of this happening in our time and
place. In 2019, *The New York Times*, the world's most influential
newspaper, launched the "1619 Project," a massive attempt to "re-
frame" (the *Times*'s word) American history by displacing the 1776
Declaration of Independence as the traditional founding of the
United States, replacing it with the year the first African slaves arrived in North America.[15]

No serious person denies the importance of slavery in US history. But that's not the point of the 1619 Project. Its goal is to revise

America's national identity by making race hatred central to the nation's foundational myth. Despite the project's core claim (that the patriots fought the American Revolution to preserve slavery) having been thoroughly debunked, journalism's elite saw fit to award the project's director a Pulitzer Prize for her contribution. Equipped with this matchless imprimatur of establishment respectability, the 1619 Project, which has already been taught in forty-five hundred classrooms,[16] will find its way into many more.

Propaganda helps change the world by creating a false impression of the way the world is. Writes Arendt, "The force possessed by totalitarian propaganda—before the movement has the power to drop the iron curtains to prevent anyone's disturbing, by the slightest reality, the gruesome quiet of an entirely imaginary world—lies in its ability to shut the masses off from the real world."[17]

In 2019, Zach Goldberg, a political science PhD student at Georgia Tech, did a deep dive on LexisNexis, the world's largest database of publicly available documents, including media reports. He found that over a nine-year period, the rate of news stories using progressive jargon associated with left-wing critical theory and social justice concepts shot into the stratosphere.[18]

What does this mean? That the mainstream media is framing the general public's understanding of news and events according to what was until very recently a radical ideology confined to left-wing intellectual elites.

It must be conceded that right-wing media, though outside the mainstream, often has a similar effect on conservatives: affirming to them that what they believe about the world is true. For all users of social media—including the nearly three quarters of US adults who use Facebook and the 22 percent who use Twitter—reinforcement of prior political beliefs is built into the system. We are being conditioned to accept as true whatever feels right to us. As Arendt wrote about the pre-totalitarian masses:

> They do not believe in anything visible, in the reality of their own experience; they do not trust their eyes and ears but only their imaginations, which may be caught by anything that is at once universal and consistent with itself. What convinces masses are not facts, and not even invented facts, but only the consistency of the system of which they are presumably part.[19]

A MANIA FOR IDEOLOGY

Why are people so willing to believe demonstrable lies? The desperation alienated people have for a story that helps them make sense of their lives and tells them what to do explains it. For a man desperate to believe, totalitarian ideology is more precious than life itself.

"He may even be willing to help in his own prosecution and frame his own death sentence if only his status as a member of the movement is not touched," Arendt wrote. Indeed, the files of the 1930s Stalinist show trials are full of false confessions by devout communists who were prepared to die rather than admit that communism was a lie.

Totalitarianism's most dedicated servants are often idealists, at least at first. Margolius Kovály testifies that she and her husband embraced communism at first precisely because it was so idealistic. It gave those who had walked out of hell a vision of paradise in which they could believe.

One of contemporary progressivism's commonly used phrases—*the personal is political*—captures the totalitarian spirit, which seeks to infuse all aspects of life with political consciousness. Indeed, the Left pushes its ideology ever deeper into the personal realm, leaving fewer and fewer areas of daily life uncontested. This, warned Arendt, is a sign that a society is ripening for totalitarianism, because that is what totalitarianism essentially is: the politicization of everything.

Infusing every aspect of life with ideology was a standard aspect of Soviet totalitarianism. Early in the Stalin era, N. V. Krylenko, a Soviet commissar (political officer), steamrolled over chess players who wanted to keep politics out of the game.

"We must finish once and for all with the neutrality of chess," he said. "We must condemn once and for all the formula 'chess for the sake of chess,' like the formula 'art for art's sake.' We must organize shockbrigades of chess-players, and begin immediate realization of a Five-Year Plan for chess."[20]

A SOCIETY THAT VALUES LOYALTY MORE THAN EXPERTISE

"Totalitarianism in power invariably replaces all first-rate talents, regardless of their sympathies, with those crackpots and fools whose lack of intellect and creativity is still the best guarantee of their loyalty," wrote Arendt.[21]

All politicians prize loyalty, but few would regard it as the most important quality in government, and even fewer would admit it. But President Donald Trump is a rule-breaker in many ways. He once said, "I value loyalty above everything else—more than brains, more than drive, and more than energy."[22]

Trump's exaltation of personal loyalty over expertise is discreditable and corrupting. But how can liberals complain? Loyalty to the group or the tribe is *at the core* of leftist identity politics. Loyalty to an ideology over expertise is no less disturbing than loyalty to a personality. This is at the root of "cancel culture," in which transgressors, however minor their infractions, find themselves cast into outer darkness.

In early 2020, an astonishing cancel-culture controversy emerged in which Jeanine Cummins, author of a much-anticipated novel about the Mexican immigrant experience, suffered savage attack in the media from some progressive Latino writers who accused the white woman of stealing the experiences of Latinos. Some prominent Latinas who had praised the book in advance of its publication—including novelist Erika L. Sanchez, and actress Salma Hayek—withdrew their backing, lest they seem disloyal to their group.

Beyond cancel culture, which is reactive, institutions are embedding within their systems ideological tests to weed out dissenters. At universities within the University of California system, for example, teachers who want to apply for tenure-track positions have to affirm their commitment to "equity, diversity, and inclusion"—and to have demonstrated it, even if it has nothing to do with their field. Similar politically correct loyalty oaths are required at leading public and private schools.

De facto loyalty tests to diversity ideology are common in corporate America. As the inventor of JavaScript, Brendan Eich was one of the most important early figures of the internet. But in 2014, he was forced out of leadership of Mozilla, the company he founded, after employees objected to a small donation he made to the 2008 campaign to stop gay marriage in California.

A Soviet-born US physician told me—after I agreed not to use his name—that he never posts anything remotely controversial on social media, because he knows that the human resources department at his hospital monitors employee accounts for evidence of disloyalty to the progressive "diversity and inclusion" creed.

That same doctor disclosed that social justice ideology is forcing physicians like him to ignore their medical training and judgment when it comes to transgender health. He said it is not permissible within his institution to advise gender-dysphoric patients against treatments they desire, even when a physician believes it is not in that particular patient's health interest.

Intellectuals Are the Revolutionary Class

In our populist era, politicians and talk-radio polemicists can rile up a crowd by denouncing elites. Nevertheless, in most societies, intellectual and cultural elites determine its long-term direction. "[*T*]*he key actor in history is not individual genius but rather the network* and the new institutions that are created out of those networks," writes sociologist James Davison Hunter.[23] Though a revolutionary idea might emerge from the masses, says Hunter, "it does not gain traction until it is embraced and propagated by elites" working through their "well-developed networks and powerful institutions."[24]

This is why it is critically important to keep an eye on intellectual discourse. Those who do not will leave the gates unguarded. As the Polish dissident and émigré Czesław Miłosz put it, "It was only toward the middle of the twentieth century that the inhabitants of many European countries came, in general unpleasantly, to the realization that their fate could be influenced directly by intricate and abstruse books of philosophy."[25]

Arendt warns that the twentieth-century totalitarian experience shows how a determined and skillful minority can come to rule over an indifferent and disengaged majority. In our time, most people regard the politically correct insanity of campus radicals as not worthy of attention. They mock them as "snowflakes" and "social justice warriors."

This is a serious mistake. In radicalizing the broader class of elites, social justice warriors (SJWs) are playing a similar historic role to the Bolsheviks in prerevolutionary Russia. SJW ranks are full of middle-class, secular, educated young people wracked by guilt and anxiety over their own privilege, alienated from their own traditions, and desperate to identify with something, or someone, to give them a sense of wholeness and purpose. For them, the ideology of social justice—as defined not by church teaching but by critical theorists in the academy—functions as a pseudoreligion. Far from being confined to campuses and dry intellectual journals, SJW ideals are transforming elite institutions and networks of power and influence.

The social justice cultists of our day are pale imitations of Lenin and his fiery disciples. Aside from the ruthless antifa faction, they restrict their violence to words and bullying within bourgeois institutional contexts. They prefer to push around college administrators, professors, and white-collar professionals. Unlike the Bolsheviks, who were hardened revolutionaries, SJWs get their way not by shedding blood but by shedding tears.

Yet there are clear parallels—parallels that those who once lived under communism can identify.

Like the early Bolsheviks, SJWs are radically alienated from society. They too believe that justice depends on group identity, and that achieving justice means taking power away from the exploiters and handing it to the exploited.

Social justice cultists, like the first Bolsheviks, are intellectuals whose gospel is spread by intellectual agitation. It is a gospel that depends on awakening and inspiring hatred in the hearts of those it wishes to induce into revolutionary consciousness. This is why it matters immensely that they have established their base within universities, where they can indoctrinate in spiteful ideology those who will be going out to work in society's institutions.

As Russia's Marxist revolutionaries did, our own SJWs believe that science is on their side, even when their claims are unscientific. For example, transgender activists insist that their radical beliefs are scientifically sound; scientists and physicians who disagree are driven out of their institutions or intimidated into silence.

Social justice cultists are utopians who believe that the ideal of Progress requires smashing all the old forms for the sake of liberating humanity. Unlike their Bolshevik predecessors, they don't want to seize the means of economic production but rather the means of cultural production. They believe that after humanity is freed from the chains that bind us—whiteness, patriarchy, marriage, the gender binary, and so on—we will experience a radically new and improved form of life.

Finally, unlike the Bolsheviks, who wanted to destroy and replace the institutions of Russian society, our social justice warriors adopt a later Marxist strategy for bringing about social change: marching through the institutions of bourgeois society, conquering them, and using them to transform the world. For example, when the LGBT cause was adopted by corporate America as part of its branding strategy, its ultimate victory was assured.

Futuristic Fatalism

To be sure, neither loneliness, nor social atomization, nor the rise of social justice radicalism among power-holding elites—none of this means that totalitarianism is inevitable. But they do signify that the weaknesses in contemporary American society are consonant with a pre-totalitarian state.

Like the imperial Russians, we Americans may well be living in a fog of self-deception about our own country's stability. To recap:

Faith in most major institutions has declined sharply. Politics are so divided by rigid ideologies that it is difficult for the US federal government to get anything done. Participation in civic life is cratering. As the state drowns in oceans of debt, wealth inequality is at nearly a one-hundred-year high, with the middle class shrinking.

Younger generations are abandoning religion, which binds and gives purpose to societies. Church leaders don't know how to deal with this chronic crisis; as with the out-of-touch Orthodox hierarchy and clergy of the late imperial period, many don't seem to realize what's happening, much less how to address the decay.

Pornography is ubiquitous, but marriage and family formation are petering out. Ours is also an intensely sensual age, one that emphasizes sensate experiences over spiritual and rational ideals. That sexual desire is taken to be the central fact of contemporary identity is not seriously contested (it is telling that in the irreconcilable conflict between religious liberty and gay rights, the latter is winning in a blitzkrieg). The swift acceptance of gender ideology is a clear sign that Prometheanism and sensualism have been joined and have overturned the old order. The internet has acculturated at least one generation to pornography, far exceeding anything that those who overturned Russia's censorship law in 1905 could have envisioned.

The Prometheanism that drove prerevolutionary Russians predominates in twenty-first-century America. As inhabitants of the quintessential modern nation, Americans have always celebrated science, technology, and the self-made man. Today Silicon Valley is our dream factory, generating spectacular wealth and manufacturing belief in utopian change through advanced technologies.

A collapse, followed by revolutionary reconstruction, could happen much faster than we think. As Dr. Silvester Krčméry, one of Father Kolaković's disciples, put it:

> We live, contented and safe, with the idea that in a civilized country, in the mostly cultured and democratic environment of our times, such a coercive regime is impossible. We forget that in unstable countries, a certain political structure can lead to indoctrination and terror, where individual elements and stages of brainwashing are already implemented. This, at first, is quite inconspicuous. However, often in a very short time, it can develop into a full undemocratic totalitarian system.[26]

It only takes a catalyst like war, economic depression, plague, or some other severe and prolonged crisis that brings the legitimacy of the liberal democratic system into question. As Arendt warned more than half a century ago:

> There is a great temptation to explain away the intrinsically incredible by means of liberal rationalizations. In

each one of us, there lurks such a liberal, wheedling us with the voice of common sense. The road to totalitarian domination leads through many intermediate stages for which we can find numerous analogues and precedents. . . . What common sense and "normal people" refuse to believe is that everything is possible.[27]

Social justice warriors and the theorists of their cause are not "normal people" who live by common sense. Fanatical belief in Progress is a driving force behind their febrile utopianism. The ideology of progress, which has been with us in various forms since the Enlightenment, explains their confident zealotry. It also explains why so many ordinary people who aren't especially engaged by politics find it hard to say no to SJW demands. We cannot understand the hypnotic allure of left-wing totalitarianism or figure out how best to resist its advocates unless we grasp its most dedicated advocates as cultists devoted to the Myth of Progress.

CHAPTER THREE

Progressivism as Religion

People fascinated by the idea of progress never suspect that
every step forward is also a step on the way to the end.

MILAN KUNDERA, *THE BOOK OF*
LAUGHTER AND FORGETTING[1]

n 1905, Moscow high society gave a banquet in honor of the
Russian arts impresario Sergei Diaghilev at the Hotel Metropol
in Moscow. Diaghilev had recently curated an epic Saint Petersburg exhibition of portraits he had selected on an exhaustive tour
of private homes of the wealthy. The dinner was to celebrate his
success. Diaghilev knew that Russia was on the precipice of something big. He rose and delivered this toast:

> We are witnesses of the greatest moment of summing-up in
> history, in the name of a new and unknown culture, which

will be created by us, and which will also sweep us away. That is why, without fear or misgiving, I raise my glass to the ruined walls of the beautiful palaces, as well as to the new commandments of a new aesthetic. The only wish that I, an incorrigible sensualist, can express, is that the forthcoming struggle should not damage the amenities of life, and that the death should be as beautiful and as illuminating as the resurrection.[2]

What Russia's young artists, intellectuals, and cultural elite hoped for and expected was the end of autocracy, class division, and religion, and the advent of a world of liberalism, equality, and secularism. What they got instead was dictatorship, gulags, and the extermination of free speech and expression. Communists had sold their ideology to gullible optimists as the fullest version of the thing every modern person wanted: Progress.

The modern age is built on the Myth of Progress. By "myth," I mean that the concept of historical progress is foundational to the modern era and built into the story we tell ourselves to understand our time and our place in it. Believers in the Myth of Progress hold that the present is better than the past, and that the future will *inevitably* be better than the present.

This myth is a powerful tool in the hands of would-be totalitarians. It provides a transcendent source of legitimacy for their actions, and frames opposition as backward and ignorant. Understanding how communists manipulated the Myth of Progress is important to grasping how today's progressives roll over the opposition.

The Grand March

Those steeped in the teachings of Marx believed that communism was inevitable because History—a force with godlike powers of determination—required it. Kundera says that what makes a leftist (of any kind—socialists, communists, Trotskyites, left-liberals, and so on) a leftist is a shared belief that humanity is on a "Grand March" toward Progress: "The Grand March is the splendid march on the road to brotherhood, equality, justice, happiness; it goes on and on, obstacles notwithstanding, for obstacles there must be if the march is to be the Grand March."[3]

If progress is inevitable, and the Communist Party is the leader of society's Grand March to the progressive future, then, the theory goes, to resist the Party is to stand against the future —indeed, against reality itself. Those who oppose the Party oppose progress and freedom and align themselves with greed, backwardness, bigotry, and all manner of injustice. How necessary—indeed, how noble—it is of the Party to bulldoze these stumbling blocks on the Grand March and make straight and smooth the road to tomorrow.

"There was constant propaganda about how communism was changing the village for the better," recalls Tamás Sályi, a Budapest teacher of English, of his Hungarian youth. "There were always films of the farmer learning to improve his life with new technology. Those who rejected it were [depicted as] endangering their families. There are so many examples about how everything old and traditional prevented life from being good and happy."

Thus does the Myth of Progress become a justification for exercising dictatorial power to eliminate all opposition. Today, totalitarianism amounts to strict, forced regimentation of the Grand

March toward Progress. It is the method by which true believers in Progress aim to keep all of society moving forward toward utopia in lockstep, both in their outward actions and in their innermost thoughts.

Modernity Is Progress

Alas, devotion to the ideal of Progress did not begin with Marx and is not limited to Marxists. The most ardent suburban Republican is as much a believer in the Myth of Progress as the most ideologically rigid faculty Trotskyist. As historian Yuri Slezkine writes, "[F]aith in progress is just as basic to modernity as the Second Coming was to Christianity."[4]

What separates classical liberals (of both the Left and the Right) from socialists and communists is the ultimate goal toward which we are progressing, and the degree to which they believe the state should involve itself in guiding that progress. Classical liberals are more concerned with individual freedom, while leftists embrace equality of outcome. And classical liberals favor a more or less limited role for the government, while leftists believe that achieving their vision of justice and virtue requires a heavier state hand.

President Barack Obama nodded to the Myth of Progress when he cited a line popularized by Martin Luther King Jr.: "The arc of the moral universe is long, but it bends toward justice." In his second inaugural address, President George W. Bush expressed his faith in it when he declared that the United States is a vanguard of global liberal democracy.

"There is only one force of history that can break the reign of hatred and resentment," he said, "and expose the pretensions of tyrants, and reward the hopes of the decent and tolerant, and that is the force of human freedom."[5]

Bush's war to liberate Iraq for liberal democracy failed, but drinking deeply of that intoxicating rhetoric makes it easy for Americans to forget these things. It's not necessarily because we are foolish; the Myth of Progress is written into our cultural DNA. Perhaps no country on earth has been more future-oriented than the United States of America. We are suckers for the Myth of Progress —but to be fair, we have reason to be.

Over the relatively short period of our nation's history, and after hard struggles, liberal democracy and capitalism have created one of the world's highest standards of living, and have guaranteed civil rights and expanded personal freedom to all. Within living memory, black Americans were forbidden in some parts of the country from voting or eating at the same restaurants as whites. That ended, in large part because the US federal government finally acted to make the Constitution's promises good for black Americans too. Sometimes, progress is real and tangible.

We also believe in progress because of its Judeo-Christian roots. Most ancient cultures have a cyclical view of history, but Hebrew religion—and its offshoots, Christianity and Islam—describe history as moving in a linear direction, from creation to an ultimate redemption. In Christianity, that redemption will come after the Apocalypse and Last Judgment, in which God's justice will triumph.

Again, progress can be real, and for Christians at least, history is moving toward a glorious end (after a violent apocalypse), but this does not mean that all changes improve upon the past inevitably. It also doesn't mean that "progress" divorced from God is progress at all. In fact, progress can become very dark in a secular context, without a biblical understanding of human fallibility and without the God of the Bible as the author of history and the judge of the earth.

Today's progressivism dates back to the eighteenth-century Enlightenment, when its more radical Continental exponents secularized Christian hope by replacing faith in God with faith in man—particularly science and technology. Henri de Saint-Simon (1760–1825) was a French thinker who became one of the founders of socialism. Saint-Simon and his comrade Auguste Comte (1798–1857) were exponents of positivism, a philosophy built on the idea that science was the source of all authoritative knowledge.

Positivists believed that history was primarily the story of the advance of science and technology. They believed that science would eventually end all material suffering. And as science advanced, so too would morality, because it would be based on scientific knowledge, not religion and custom.

In England, philosopher John Stuart Mill (1806–1873) incorporated positivism into the classical liberal political tradition. In Germany, Karl Marx put it to use in building a radical politics. Marx and his disciples replaced the Christian hope in a reward in heaven with the belief that perfection could—and inevitably would—be established on this earth, after a savage apocalypse, and through the application of science and science-based politics.

Though Marxists took positivism in an extreme, utopian direction, positivist values are at the foundation of free-market liberalism. Both traditions believe that science drives progress and that progress can be measured by the alleviation of material needs.

Contemporary philosopher John Gray says that there is much less distance between liberal democrats and Marxists than we like to think: "Technology—the practical application of scientific knowledge—produces a convergence in values. This is the central modern myth which the Positivists propagated and everyone today accepts as fact."[6]

The original American dream—the one held by the seventeenth-century Puritan settlers—was religious: to establish liberty as the condition that allowed them to worship and to serve God as dictated by their consciences. In our time, the American dream is not a religious ideal but rather one informed more by positivism than Christianity. For most people, the term means wealth and material stability and the freedom to create the life that one desires. The Puritan ideal was to use freedom to live by virtue, as defined by Christian Scripture; the modern American ideal is to use freedom to achieve well-being, as defined by the sacred individual—that is, a Self that is fully the product of choice and consent. The Myth of Progress teaches that science and technology will empower individuals, unencumbered by limits imposed by religion and tradition, to realize their desires.

In modern politics, anyone who can be portrayed as an opponent of progress is often at a disadvantage. To oppose progress, to be against change, is to stand against the natural order of things. In liberal democracies, the struggle between the Right and the Left is really a contest between conservative progressives and radical progressives over the rate and details of change. What is not in dispute is the shared belief that the good society is one in which individuals have enough money and personal autonomy to do whatever they like.

Progress as Religion

For classical liberal devotees of the Myth of Progress, the ideal society is one in which everyone has equal freedom of choice. For radicals, it is one in which everyone is living with equality of outcome. Belief that one's circumstances can be improved by collective human effort, though, is a powerful political motivator. It is difficult to see this from the perspective of the twenty-first century, but to believe that poverty, sickness, and oppression are not destined to be one's fate was a revolutionary concept in human history. It gave people whose ancestors had scarcely known anything but want and suffering hope for the future.

Marx likened religion to a drug because it blunted the pain of life for the masses, and in his view, took away from them the consciousness that they had the power to overturn the social order that immiserated them. Unlike progressives in the classical liberal tradition, Marx and his fellow radicals promised that radical politics, harnessing the power of science and technology, really could establish heaven on earth. They were atheists who believed that man could become like a god.

As a perversion of religion, Progress as an ideology speaks appealingly to hungry human hearts. As Miłosz and other dissidents testify, communism answered an essentially religious longing in the souls of restless young intellectuals. Progressivism in all its forms appeals to the same desire in intelligent young people today—both secular and those within churches who are alienated from authoritative ecclesial traditions. This is why Christians today must understand that, fundamentally, they aren't resisting a different politics but rather what is effectively a rival religion.

This is how it was for young Russians of the late nineteenth century, who embraced Marxism with the fervor of religious converts. It gave its devotees a narrative that helped them understand why things are the way they are, and what they, as Marxists, should do to bring about a more just world. It was an optimistic philosophy, one that promised relief and bounty for all the peoples of the world.

To create utopia, Marxists first had to rout Christianity, which they saw as a false religion that sanctified the ruling class and kept the poor superstitious and easy to control. The Russian radicals also hated the so-called Philistines—their word for the deplorable people who live out their daily lives without thinking of anything higher or greater. The radical intelligentsia regarded the Philistines as their complete opposites: the rough and beastly Goliaths to their clever Davids. They hated the Philistines with all-consuming intensity—no doubt partly because so many of them had come from such families.

The comfortable Philistines were not the kind of people prepared to suffer and die for their beliefs. The Bolsheviks were. The tsarist government sent many of their leaders into Siberian exile, which did not break them but made them stronger.

"Exile stood for suffering, intimacy, and the sublime immensity of the heavenly depths. It offered a perfect metaphor for both what was wrong with the 'world of lies' and what was central to the promise of socialism," writes Yuri Slezkine.[7] To be a revolutionary in those days was to share a sense of purpose, of community, of hope—and an electrifying bond of contempt, a contempt we see in the social justice movement today toward anyone who differs from its religious claims.

As Slezkine has said, both the Christian faith and totalitarianism share an ultimate concern with the inner man. Christianity and communism—which is to say, the most radical form of progressivism—are best understood as competing religions. Despite the self-delusions of theologically progressive Christians, so too are Christianity and the easygoing nihilism that characterizes progressivism in our post-Christian era.

Heresy-Hunters in Our Midst

In 2019, I went to see the English public intellectual Sir Roger Scruton, in what turned out to be the last summer of his life, because of his work in the 1980s supporting dissidents in Eastern Europe. He was instrumental in helping to establish an underground university in Prague. As Britain's best-known conservative academic, he subsequently emerged as one of the most penetrating and articulate critics of what we call "political correctness"—in part because he has so often been its victim.

Settling into his farmhouse library in rural Wiltshire, Sir Roger agreed that we are not waging a political battle but are rather engaged in a war of religion. "There is no official line in this, but it all congeals around a set of doctrines which we don't have any problem in recognizing."

He explained that in the emerging soft totalitarianism, any thought or behavior that can be identified as excluding members of groups favored by the Left is subject to harsh condemnation. This "official doctrine" is not imposed from above by the regime but rather arises by left-wing consensus from below, along with severe enforcement in the form of witch-hunting and scapegoating.

"If you step out of line, especially if you're in the area of opinion-forming as a journalist or an academic, then the aim is to prevent your voice from being heard," said Scruton. "So, you'll be thrown out of whatever teaching position you have or, like me recently, made the topic of a completely mendacious fabricated interview used to accuse you of all the thoughtcrimes."

Scruton was referring to a left-wing journalist to whom he had recently granted an interview. The journalist twisted Scruton's words to make him sound like a bigot and crowed on social media that he had taken the scalp of a "racist and homophobe." Fortunately, a recording of the interview emerged and vindicated Sir Roger. Many others in our time who are accused of similar thoughtcrimes—Orwell's term for ideological offenses—are not so lucky.

Scruton told me that thoughtcrimes—heresies, in other words—by their very nature make accusation and guilt the same thing. He saw this in his travels in the communist world, where the goal was to keep the system in place with minimal effort.

"For this purpose, there were thoughtcrimes invented every now and then with which to trap the enemy of the people," he said. "In my day it was the 'Zionist Imperialist Conspiracy.' You could be accused of being a member of that, and nobody could possibly find a defense against the accusation because nobody knew what it was!

"It's just like 'homophobia' or 'Islamophobia,' these new thoughtcrimes," Scruton continued. "What on earth do they mean? And then everyone can join in the throwing of electronic stones at the scapegoat and never be held to account for it, because you don't have to prove the accusation."

The reach of contemporary thoughtcrime expands constantly—homophobia, Islamophobia, transphobia, bi-phobia, fat-phobia, racism, ableism, and on and on—making it difficult to know when one is treading on safe ground or about to step on a land mine. Yet Scruton is right: All of these thoughtcrimes derive from "doctrines"—his word—that are familiar to all of us. These doctrines inform the ideological thrust behind the soft totalitarianism of our own time as surely as Marxist doctrines of economic class struggle did the hard totalitarianism of the Soviet era.

One imagines an entry-level worker at a Fortune 500 firm, or an untenured university lecturer, suffering through the hundredth workshop on Diversity, Equity, and Inclusion and doing their very best not to be suspected of dissent. In fact, I don't have to imagine it at all. As a journalist who writes about these issues, I often hear stories from people—always white-collar professionals like academics, doctors, lawyers, engineers—who live closeted lives as religious or social conservatives. They know that to dissent from the progressive regime in the workplace, or even to be suspected of dissent, would likely mean burning their careers at the stake.

For example, an American academic who has studied Russian communism told me about being present at the meeting in which his humanities department decided to require from job applicants a formal statement of loyalty to the ideology of diversity—even though this has nothing to do with teaching ability or scholarship.

The professor characterized this as a McCarthyite way of eliminating dissenters from the employment pool, and putting those already on staff on notice that they will be monitored for deviation from the social-justice party line.

That is a soft form of totalitarianism. Here is the same logic laid down hard: in 1918, Lenin unleashed the Red Terror, a campaign of annihilation against those who resisted Bolshevik power. Martin

Latsis, head of the secret police in Ukraine, instructed his agents as follows:

> Do not look in the file of incriminating evidence to see whether or not the accused rose up against the Soviets with arms or words. Ask him instead to which class he belongs, what is his background, his education, his profession. These are the questions that will determine the fate of the accused. That is the meaning and essence of the Red Terror.[8]

Note well that an individual's words and deeds had nothing to do with determining one's guilt or innocence. One was presumed guilty based entirely on one's class and social status. A revolution that began as an attempt to right historical injustices quickly became an exterminationist exercise of raw power. Communists justified the imprisonment, ruin, and even the execution of people who stood in the way of Progress as necessary to achieve historical justice over alleged exploiters of privilege.

A softer, bloodless form of the same logic is at work in American institutions. Social justice progressives advance their malignant concept of justice in part by terrorizing dissenters as thoroughly as any inquisitor on the hunt for enemies of religious orthodoxy.

Understanding the Cult of Social Justice

In the last chapter, we briefly examined how social justice warriors play a similar role in our society that Bolsheviks played in late imperial Russia, and sketched a profile of the typical SJW. Perhaps no public intellectual has thought so deeply about the fundamentally religious nature of these progressive militants than James A. Lindsay, an atheist and university mathematician.

Lindsay contends that social justice fulfills the same psychological and social needs that religion once filled but no longer can. And like conventional religions, it depends on axiomatic claims that cannot be falsified but only accepted as revealed truths. This is why arguments with these zealots are about as productive as theological disputation with a synod of Taliban divines. For the social justice inquisitors, "dialogue" is the process by which opponents confess their sins and submit in fear and trembling to the social justice creed.

Social justice warriors are members of what Lindsay calls an "ideologically motivated moral community." Far from being moral relativists, SJWs truly are rigorists with a deep and abiding concern for purity, and they do not hesitate to enforce their sacrosanct beliefs. Those beliefs give meaning and direction to their lives and provide a sense of shared mission.

What are those beliefs? A rough catechism based on Lindsay's analysis[9] goes something like this.

THE CENTRAL FACT OF HUMAN EXISTENCE IS POWER AND HOW IT IS USED

Politics is the art and science of how power is distributed and exercised in a society. For SJWs, everything in life is understood through relationships of power. Social justice is the mission of reordering society to create more equitable (just) power relationships. Those who resist social justice are practicing "hate," and cannot be reasoned with or in any way tolerated, only conquered.

THERE IS NO SUCH THING AS OBJECTIVE TRUTH; THERE IS ONLY POWER

Who decides what is true and what is false? Those who hold power. Religious claims, philosophical arguments, political theories—all of these are veils concealing will to power. They are only rationalizations for oppressors to hold power over the oppressed. The value of truth claims depends on who is making them.

IDENTITY POLITICS SORTS OPPRESSED FROM OPPRESSORS

In classic Marxism, the bourgeoisie are the oppressor, and the proletariat are the oppressed. In the cult of social justice, the oppressors are generally white, male, heterosexual, and Christian. The oppressed are racial minorities, women, sexual minorities, and religious minorities. (Curiously, the poor are relatively low on the hierarchy of oppression. For example, a white Pentecostal man living on disability in a trailer park is an oppressor; a black lesbian Ivy League professor is oppressed.) Justice is not a matter of working out what is rightly due to an individual per se, but what is due to an individual as the bearer of a group identity.

INTERSECTIONALITY IS SOCIAL JUSTICE ECUMENISM

People who bear identities within the so-called "matrix of oppression" link their identities to one another by way of intersectionality. The concept is that all those oppressed by the privileged classes—the patriarchy, whiteness, and so forth—are connected by virtue of their oppression and should challenge power as a united front. If one is not a member of an oppressed group, he or she can become an "ally" in the power struggle.

LANGUAGE CREATES HUMAN REALITIES

Social justice warriors believe that human nature is constructed largely through the use of linguistic conventions. This is why they focus heavily on "discourses"—that is, the style and content of modes of speaking that, in their view, legitimize certain ways of being and delegitimize others. SJWs tightly police the spoken and written word, condemning speech that offends them as a form of violence.

Conservatives, old-fashioned liberals, and others who are outside the social justice movement frequently fail to grasp how to respond to the aggressive claims of its proponents. This is because they assume SJWs, who are typically not religious, operate under the established standards of secular liberal discourse, with its respect for discursive reasoning.

A memorable example is the 2015 Yale University clash between professors Nicholas and Erika Christakis and enraged students from the residential college overseen by the faculty couple. Things went very badly for the Christakises, old-school liberals who erred by thinking that the students could be engaged with the tools and procedures of reason. Alas, the students were in the grip of the religion of social justice. As such, they considered their subjective beliefs to be a form of uncontestable knowledge, and disagreement as an attack on their identity.

Some conservatives think that SJWs should be countered with superior arguments and if conservatives stick with liberal proceduralism they will prevail. This is a fundamental error that blinds conservatives to the radical nature of the threat. You cannot know how to judge and act in the face of these challenges if you cannot see the social justice warriors for what they truly are—and where they do their work. It is easy to identify the shrieking student on the university quad, but it is more important to be able to spot the subversive presence of older SJWs and fellow travelers throughout institutional bureaucracies, where they exercise immense power.

SOCIAL JUSTICE AND CHRISTIANITY

The term *social justice* has long been associated with Christianity, especially Catholic Christianity (the term was coined by a nineteenth-century Jesuit), though now it has been embraced by younger Evangelicals. In Catholic social teaching, "social justice" is the idea that individuals have a responsibility to work for the common good, so that all can live up to their dignity as creatures fashioned in God's image. In the traditional view, social justice is about addressing structural barriers to fairness among groups in a given society. It is based in large part on Christ's teachings about the importance of mercy and compassion to the poor and the outcast.

But Christian social justice is difficult to reconcile with secular ideals of social justice. One reason is that the former depends on the biblical concept of what a human being is—including the purpose for which all people were created. This presumes a transcendent moral order, proclaimed in Scripture and, depending on one's confession, the authoritative teachings of the church. A just social order is one that makes it easier for people to be good.

Peter Maurin, cofounder of the Catholic Worker movement, was a truly Christian social justice warrior. (Interestingly, Father Kolaković introduced Maurin's writing to his Family in Bratislava.) Maurin distinguished Christian social justice from the godless Marxist view. For Marxists, social justice meant an equal distribution of society's material goods. By contrast, Christian social justice sought to create conditions of unity that enabled all people—rich and poor alike—to live in solidarity and mutual charity as pilgrims on the road to unity with Christ.

In our time, secular social justice has been shorn of its Christian dimension. Because they defend a particular code of sexual morality and gender categories, Christians are seen by progressives as the enemies of social justice. Catholic philosopher Michael Hanby insightfully links sexual radicalism to the scientific roots of the Myth of Progress. He has written that "the sexual revolution is, at bottom, the technological revolution and its perpetual war against natural limits applied externally to the body and internally to our self-understanding."[10]

Without Christianity and its belief in the fallibility of human nature, secular progressives tend to rearrange their bigotries and call it righteousness. Christianity teaches that all men and women—not just the wealthy, the powerful, the straight, the white, and all other so-called oppressors—are sinners in need of the Redeemer. All men and women are called to confession and repentance. "Social justice" that projects unrighteousness solely onto particular groups is a perversion of Christian teaching. Reducing the individual to her economic status or her racial, sexual, or gender identity is an anthropological error. It is untrue, and therefore unjust.

Moreover, for Christians, no social order that denies sin, erecting structures or approving practices that alienate man from his Creator, can ever be just. Contrary to secular social justice activists, protecting the right to abortion is always unjust. So is any proposal—like same-sex marriage—that ratifies sin and undermines the natural family. In a 1986 encyclical, Pope John Paul II denounced a "spirit of darkness" that deceitfully posits "God as an enemy of his own creature, and in the first place as an enemy of man, as a source of danger and threat to man."[11]

Christians cannot endorse any form of social justice that denies biblical teaching. That includes schemes that apply identity politics categories to the life of the church. For example, answering calls to "decolonize" the church means imposing identity politics categories onto theology and worship, turning the faith into radical leftism at prayer.

Faithful Christians must work for social justice, but can only do so in the context of fidelity to the full Christian moral and theological vision through which we understand the meaning of justice. Any social justice campaign that implies that the God of the Bible is an enemy of man and his happiness is fraudulent and must be rejected.

Back to the Future?

We have to throw away this crippling nostalgia for the future, especially the habit we Americans, a naturally optimistic people, have of assuming that everything will ultimately work out for the best. Diaghilev and the swells at that 1905 banquet had no idea that the beautiful death to which they raised their glasses was going to mean the murder of millions by the executioner's bullet and engineered famine. Diaghilev was living abroad during the Russian Revolution, but having seen what the Bolsheviks swept away, he never returned home.

On the other hand, even when facts give us little reason for optimism, we Christians must not surrender hope. Eight decades after that Moscow hotel banquet, when Mikhail Gorbachev came to power in the nearby Kremlin, enslaved peoples across the Soviet empire were not aware that the vast machinery of totalitarianism was rusted to its core and would soon collapse. In fact, Flagg Taylor, an American political scientist who studies the Czech underground, told me that not a single dissident leader he interviewed for his research expected that the fall of communism would happen in their lifetimes.

Vlado Palko, a Slovak academic who stood on the main square in Bratislava braving the police water cannons at the Candle Demonstration, was one of them. He was afraid that night in 1988, and had no reason to believe that the protest called by the underground church would have any effect. But as he told his wife before leaving their flat for the square, his dignity as a man depended on showing up to stand with his fellow Catholics, candle in hand, to pray openly for freedom.

"I thought back then that communism would last for the next thousand years," he tells me. "The truth was, it did not. And that is something for us to hope for today, under this soft tyranny of political correctness. It will end. The truth has power to end every tyranny."

Palko and the others were in good company. Nearly all Western experts, scholars who had spent a lifetime studying Soviet communism failed to predict its rapid demise. We never know when history will produce figures like Lech Walesa, Aleksandr Solzhenitsyn, Karol Wojtyla, Václav Havel, and all the lesser known heroes of the resistance. They stood up for truth and justice not out of an expectation of achievable victory in their lifetimes, but because it was the right thing to do.

You don't have to be a grizzled Cold Warrior to see that a notion of progress that depends on labor camps, police informers, and making everybody equally poor to achieve justice and equality is phony. It is much harder, though, to stand against the softer version. It seems to flow naturally from the Myth of Progress as it has been lived out in our mass consumerist democracy, which has for generations defined progress as the liberation of human desire from limits. But that is exactly what traditional Christians must do, though for many of us it will mean having to unlearn political myths that we have uncritically absorbed in a culture that until fairly recently thought and reasoned in broad Christian categories. Consider that the civil rights movement of the 1960s was led by black preachers who articulated the plight of their people in Biblical language and stories.

Those days are over, and we will not be able to take the measure of the long struggle ahead if we don't understand the essential nature of the opposition.

It regards Christians as the most significant remaining obstacles on the Grand March, bearers of the cruel and outdated beliefs that keep the people from being free and happy. Wherever we hide, they will track us, find us, and punish us if that's what it takes to make this world more perfect. This brings us to the final factor critical to understanding the radical challenge facing Christianity and discerning strategies of resistance: the power and reach of surveillance technology.

CHAPTER FOUR

Capitalism, Woke and Watchful

K amila Bendova sits in her armchair in the Prague apartment where she and her late husband, Václav, used to hold underground seminars to build up the anti-communist dissident movement. It has been thirty years since the fall of communism, but Bendova is not about to lessen her vigilance about threats to freedom. I mention to her that tens of millions of Americans have installed in their houses so-called "smart speakers" that monitor conversations for the sake of making domestic life more convenient. Kamila visibly recoils. The appalled look on her face telegraphs a clear message: *How can Americans be so gullible?*

To stay free to speak the truth, she tells me, you have to create for yourself a zone of privacy that is inviolate. She reminded me that the secret police had bugged her apartment, and that she and her family had to live with the constant awareness that the government was listening to every sound they made. The idea that anybody would welcome into their home a commercial device that records conversations and transmits them to a third party is horrifying to her. No consumer convenience is worth that risk.

"Information means power," Kamila says. "We know from our life under the totalitarian regime that if you know something about someone, you can manipulate him or her. You can use it against them. The secret police have evidence of everything like that. They could use it all against you. Anything!"

Kamila pointed out to me the scars along the living room wall of her Prague apartment where, after the end of communism, she and her husband had ripped out the wires the secret police used to bug their home. It turns out that no one in the Benda family uses smartphones or emails. Too risky, they say, even today.

Some might call this paranoia. But in light of Edward Snowden's revelations, it looks a lot more like prudence. "People think that they are safe because they haven't said anything controversial," says Kamila. "That is very naive."

After the fall of the Berlin Wall and Germany's 1990 reunification, the German government opened the vast files of the Stasi, East Germany's secret police, to its victims. None of the Soviet Bloc states had a surveillance apparatus as thorough as East Germany's, nor had any communist rivals developed a culture of snitching with roots as deep and wide in the population. Historians later discovered that vast numbers of East German citizens, with no prompting by the government, volunteered negative information about their friends and neighbors. "Across the country, people were on the lookout for divergent viewpoints, which were then branded as dangerous to the state," reported the magazine *Der Spiegel*. This practice gave the East German police state an unparalleled perspective on the private lives of its citizens.

Should totalitarianism, hard or soft, come to America, the police state would not have to establish a web of informants to keep tabs on the private lives of the people. The system we have now already does this—and most Americans are scarcely aware of its thoroughness and ubiquity.

The rapidly growing power of information technology and its ubiquitous presence in daily life immensely magnifies the ability of those who control institutions to shape society according to their ideals. Throughout the past two decades, economic and techno-logical changes—changes that occurred under liberal democratic capitalism—have given both the state and corporations surveil-lance capabilities of which Lenin and Stalin could only have dreamed. In East Germany, the populace accustomed itself to total surveillance and made snitching normal behavior—this, as part of the development of what the state called the "socialist personality," which considered privacy to be harmful. In our time and place, the willingness of people to disclose deeply personal data about themselves—either actively, on platforms like Facebook, or pas-sively, through online data harvesting—is creating a new kind of person: the "social media personality," who cannot imagine why privacy matters at all.

The Rise of Woke Capitalism

To Americans conditioned by the Cold War, the all-powerful state seemed the biggest threat to liberty. We grew up reading Orwell in high school and hearing news accounts of defectors from commu-nist countries who testified to the horrors of life under total gov-ernment control. Besides, American culture has always prized the lone individual who stands out from the herd. The most iconic American—the cowboy—testifies to this enduring value.

The American conservative tradition, unlike that of Europe, has been philosophically antagonistic to the state. Yet recognizing that the Soviet Union and its allies were a genuine threat, postwar conservatives resigned themselves, putting up with big government as a necessary evil to protect American freedom.

But they didn't have to like it. To many on the Right, especially libertarians schooled by the novels of Ayn Rand, corporations seemed the natural opponent of the leviathan state. As institutions of private enterprise, corporations were seen by conservatives as more naturally virtuous than the state. The Cold War might have compelled conservatives to make peace with Big Government, but they were willing to accept Big Business as a bulwark against a too-powerful state—and on the global front, as an important weapon in advancing American soft power against Soviet hegemony.

Though liberals are less inclined to sanctify business than conservatives, the end of the Cold War brought about the conversion of leading liberal politicians—think Bill Clinton and Tony Blair—to the gospel of market globalization, already fervently accepted by all but a cranky fringe of Republicans. Over the past quarter century, globalization and technological advances have enabled a staggering expansion of corporate power.

Now an elite club of global megacorporations are more powerful than many countries. Walmart has more annual revenue than Spain and more than twice as much as Russia. ExxonMobil is bigger, revenuewise, than India, Norway, or Turkey. As international strategist Parag Khanna says, in a world where Apple has more cash on hand than two thirds of the world's nations, "corporations are likely to overtake all states in terms of clout."[1] In an

72

America that now runs on the internet, five companies—Facebook, Apple, Amazon, Microsoft, Google—have an almost incalculable influence over public and private life.

At the same time, Big Business has moved steadily leftward on social issues. Standard business practice long required staying out of controversial issues on the grounds that taking sides in the culture war would be bad for business. That all changed in a big way in 2015, when the state of Indiana passed a religious freedom bill that would have given some protection to businesses sued for anti-gay discrimination. A powerful coalition of corporate leaders, including the heads of Apple, Salesforce, Eli Lilly, and others, threatened economic retaliation against the state if it did not reverse course. It did. Since then, lobbyists for national and international corporations have leaned heavily on state governments to pass pro-LGBT legislation and to resist religious liberty laws.

The stereotype that college students leave their liberalism behind on campus when they graduate into the "real world" is badly outdated. In fact, today's graduates are often taught to bring their social justice ideals with them and advocate for what is called "corporate social responsibility." True, nobody has a good word to say for corporate social irresponsibility; like "social justice," the phrase is a euphemism for a progressive cultural politics. As author Heather Mac Donald has written, "[G]raduates of the academic victimology complex are remaking the world in their image."[2]

In her 2018 book, *The Diversity Delusion*, Mac Donald explored how corporate human resources departments function as a social justice commissariat. Nearly 90 percent of Fortune 500 companies have diversity offices, she reports, and the corporate mania for "equity, diversity, and inclusion" informs corporate culture at many levels, including hiring, promotion, bonuses, and governing the norms of interaction in the workplace.

Some multinational corporations impose progressive cultural politics on workplaces in more socially conservative countries. Several Polish employees of the national branches of world-renowned corporations told me that they have felt compelled to participate in LGBT activism inside their companies. As Christians, they believed endorsing Pride violated their consciences, but given economic conditions in Poland, they feared refusing to conform would cost them their jobs.

There is nothing wrong, of course, with trying to create workplaces where people are treated fairly, and judged according to performance. That's what we call "justice"; social justice, as we have seen, is not the same thing. Mac Donald found little to no empirical evidence to support social justice strategies within the corporate world. Despite this, these supposedly hardheaded business executives ignore the bottom line when it comes to diversity programs and corporate social responsibility initiatives. It's as if these rites and catechisms were more an expression of religious belief than a response to real-world conditions.

The embrace of aggressive social progressivism by Big Business is one of the most underappreciated stories of the last two decades. Critics call it "woke capitalism," a snarky theft of the left-wing slang term indicating progressive enlightenment. Woke capitalism is now the most transformative agent within the religion of social justice, because it unites progressive ideology with the most potent force in American life: consumerism and making money.

In his 2018 letter to investors, Larry Fink, CEO of the global investment company BlackRock, said that corporate social responsibility is now part of the cost of doing business.

"Society is demanding that companies, both public and private, serve a social purpose," Fink wrote. "To prosper over time, every company must not only deliver financial performance, but also show how it makes a positive contribution to society."[3]

Poll results about consumer expectations back Fink up. Millennials and Generation Z customers are especially prone to seeing their consumer expenditures as part of creating a socially conscious personal brand identity. For many companies, then, signaling progressive virtues to consumers is a smart business move in the same way that signaling all-American patriotism would have been to corporations in the 1950s.

But what counts as a "positive contribution to society"? Corporations like to brand themselves as being in favor of a predictable constellation of causes, all of them guiding stars of the progressive cosmos. Woke capitalist branding harnesses the unmatched propaganda resources of the advertising industry to send the message, both explicitly and implicitly: the beliefs of social conservatives and religious traditionalists are obstacles to the social good.

The Rise of Surveillance Capitalism

The politicization of life in corporations along social justice lines has occurred at the same time that Big Business has embraced amassing personal data as a key sales and marketing strategy.

In Orwell's *Nineteen Eighty-Four*, Winston Smith must live with a telescreen in his apartment. The two-way device delivers propaganda but also monitors residents, allowing the totalitarian state to invade the privacy of people's homes.

Given that generations of American students have read Orwell's novel, you would think they would be inoculated against accepting this kind of invasive technology.

You would be wrong. In the twenty-first century, Big Brother has found a much more insidious way into our homes. In fact, he has been invited. Nearly 70 million Americans have one or more wireless "smart speakers"—usually manufactured by Amazon or Google—in their residences.[4] Smart speakers are voice-recognition devices connected to the internet. They serve as digital assistants, recording vocal commands, and in response, executing actions—obtaining information, ordering retail goods, controlling lights and music, and so forth. For over 25 percent of the population, convenience has overcome privacy concerns.

Consumerism is how we are learning to love Big Brother. What's more, Big Brother is not exactly who we expected him to be—a political dictator, though one day he may become that. At the present moment, Big Brother's primary occupation is capitalist. He's a salesman, he's a broker, he's a gatherer of raw materials, and a manufacturer of desires. He is monitoring virtually every move you make to determine how to sell you more things, and in so doing, learning how to direct your behavior. In this way, Big Brother is laying the foundation for soft totalitarianism, both in terms of creating and implementing the technology for political and social control and by grooming the population to accept it as normal.

This is the world of "surveillance capitalism," a term coined by Shoshana Zuboff, a former Harvard Business School professor. In her 2019 book, *The Age of Surveillance Capitalism*, Zuboff describes and analyzes a new form of capitalism created by Google and perfected by Amazon and Facebook. Surveillance capitalism hoovers up detailed personal data about individuals and analyzes it with sophisticated algorithms to predict people's behavior.

The aim, obviously, is to pitch goods and services tailored to individual preferences. No surprise there—that's merely advertising. The deeper realities of surveillance capitalism, however, are far more sinister. The masters of data aren't simply trying to figure out what you like; they are now at work making you like what they want you to like, without their manipulation being detected.

And they're doing this without the knowledge or informed permission of the people whose lives they have colonized—and who are at present without means to escape the surveillance capitalists' web. You may have given up Facebook over privacy concerns, and may have vowed never to have a smart device under your roof, but unless you are a hermit living off the grid, you are still thoroughly bounded and penetrated by the surveillance capitalist system.

"This power to shape behavior for others' profit or power is entirely self-authorizing," Zuboff told *The Guardian*. "It has no foundation in democratic or moral legitimacy, as it usurps decision rights and erodes the processes of individual autonomy that are essential to the function of a democratic society. The message here is simple: *Once I was mine. Now I am theirs* [italics added]."[5]

The story of surveillance capitalism begins in 2003, when Google, by far the world's largest internet search engine, patented a process to allow it to use the vast amount of data it gathered from individual searches in a new way. The company's data scientists had figured out how to utilize "data exhaust"—surplus information obtained from searches—to predict the kind of advertising that would most appeal to individual users.

Before long, "data extraction" became the basis for a new tech-based economy. Google, Facebook, Amazon, and others discovered how to make fortunes by gathering, packaging, and selling personal data about individuals. By now, it is not a matter of vending your name, address, and email address to third parties. It is vastly more thorough. Web-connected sensors are reporting facts and data about you constantly.

Consider this scenario: The alarm on your smartphone by your bedside buzzes you out of bed in the morning. While you were asleep, the apps on the phone uploaded the previous day's information about your activities on it to the app owner. You crawl out of bed, brush your teeth, put on your shorts and sneakers, and take a twenty-minute run around your neighborhood. The Fitbit on your wrist records your workout information and uploads it.

Back home, you shower, go into the kitchen to pour yourself a bowl of cereal, and sit down at the kitchen table to check you Gmail account, Facebook, and your favorite news and information sites. Everything you write on Gmail is processed by Google, which scans the text for key words to direct advertising to you. Everything you post, Like, or forward on Facebook is recorded by the company and used in its advertising. The company's algorithms are so sophisticated now that Facebook can make detailed predictions about you just by associating certain data points. When you scan newspaper websites, cookies embedded in your browser report back about which stories you've read.

As you drive to work, sensors in your car record and report your driving habits, because you allowed your car insurance company to capture this data in exchange for a lower rate for safe drivers. Meanwhile, the insurance company's sensors record data about which stores you stop at, and then report all that back to the insurance company, which sells that data to marketers.

All day long, the smartphone in your pocket sends data about its location—and therefore, yours—back to your service provider. You are trackable at all times—and disabling location services in your device is not foolproof. All the requests you make of Siri, your digital assistant? Recorded and monetized. All the Google searches during the day? Recorded and monetized. You go out for lunch and pay with your credit or debit card? Marketers know where you've eaten and match that data to your personal profile. Stop at the supermarket on the way home to pick up a few things and pay with the card? They know what you bought.

Your smart refrigerator is sending data about your eating habits to someone. Your smart television is doing the same thing about what you're watching. Your smart television will soon be watching you, literally. Zuboff reports on prizewinning research by a company called Realeyes that will use facial data recognition to make it possible for machines to analyze emotions using facial responses. When this technology becomes available, your smart TV (smartphone or laptop) will be able to monitor your involuntary response to commercials and other programming and report that information to outside sources. It doesn't take a George Orwell to understand the danger posed by this all-but-inescapable technology.

The Politics of Surveillance

Why should corporations and institutions not use the information they harvest to manufacture consent to some beliefs and ideologies and to manipulate the public into rejecting others?

In recent years, the most obvious interventions have come from social media companies deplatforming users for violating terms of service. Twitter and Facebook routinely boot users who violate its standards, such as promoting violence, sharing pornography, and the like. YouTube, which has two billion active users, has demonetized users who made money from their channels but who crossed the line with content YouTube deemed offensive. To be fair to these platform managers, there really are vile people who want to use these networks to advocate for evil things.

But who decides what crosses the line? Facebook bans what it calls "expression that . . . has the potential to intimidate, exclude or silence others." To call that a capacious definition is an understatement. Twitter boots users who "misgender" or "deadname" transgendered people. Calling Caitlyn Jenner "Bruce," or using masculine pronouns when referring to the transgendered celebrity, is grounds for removal.

To be sure, being kicked off of social media isn't like being sent to Siberia. But companies like PayPal have used the guidance of the far-left Southern Poverty Law Center to make it impossible for certain right-of-center individuals and organizations—including the mainstream religious-liberty law advocates Alliance Defending Freedom—to use its services.[6] Though the bank issued a general denial when asked, JPMorgan Chase has been credibly accused of closing the accounts of an activist it associates with the alt-right.[7] In 2018, Citigroup and Bank of America announced plans to stop doing some business with gun manufacturers.[8]

It is not at all difficult to imagine that banks, retailers, and service providers that have access to the kind of consumer data extracted by surveillance capitalists would decide to punish individuals affiliated with political, religious, or cultural groups those firms deem to be antisocial. Silicon Valley is well known to be far to the left on social and cultural issues, a veritable mecca of the cult of social justice. Social justice warriors are known for the spiteful disdain they hold for classically liberal values like free speech, freedom of association, and religious liberty. These are the kinds of people who will be making decisions about access to digital life and to commerce. The rising generation of corporate leaders takes pride in their progressive awareness and activism. Twenty-first-century capitalism is not only all in for surveillance, it is also very woke.

Nor is it hard to foresee these powerful corporate interests using that data to manipulate individuals into thinking and acting in certain ways. Zuboff quotes an unnamed Silicon Valley bigwig saying, "Conditioning at scale is essential to the new science of massively engineered human behavior." He believes that by close analysis of the behavior of app users, his company will eventually be able to "change how lots of people are making their day-to-day decisions."[9]

Maybe they will just try to steer users into buying certain products and not others. But what happens when the products are politicians or ideologies? And how will people know when they are being manipulated?

If a corporation with access to private data decides that progress requires suppressing dissenting opinions, it will be easy to identify the dissidents, even if they have said not one word publicly.

In fact, they may have their public voices muted. British writer Douglas Murray documented how Google quietly weights its search results to return more "diverse" findings. Though Google presents its search results as disinterested, Murray shows that "what is revealed is not a 'fair' view of things, but a view which severely skews history and presents it with a bias from the present."[10]

Result: for the search engine preferred by 90 percent of global internet users, "progress"—as defined by left-wing Westerners living in Silicon Valley—is presented as normative.

In another all-too-common example, the populist Vox party in Spain had its Twitter access temporarily suspended when, in January 2020, a politician in the Socialist Party accused the Vox party of "hate speech," for opposing the Socialist-led government's plan to force schoolchildren to study gender ideology, even if parents did not consent.

To be sure, Twitter, a San Francisco-based company with 330 million global users, especially among media and political elites, is not a publicly regulated utility; it is under no legal obligation to offer free speech to its users. But consider how it would affect everyday communications if social media and other online channels that most people have come to depend on—Twitter, Gmail, Facebook, and others—were to decide to cut off users whose religious or political views qualified them as bigots in the eyes of the digital commissars?

What is holding the government back from doing the same thing? It's not from a lack of technological capacity. In 2013, Edward Snowden, the renegade National Security Agency analyst, revealed that the US federal government's spying was vastly greater than previously known. In his 2019 memoir, *Permanent Record*, Snowden writes of learning that

> the US government was developing the capacity of an eternal law-enforcement agency. At any time, the government could dig through the past communications of anyone it wanted to victimize in search of a crime (and everybody's communications contain evidence of something). At any point, for all perpetuity, any new administration—any fu-

ture rogue head of the NSA—could just show up to work and, as easily as flicking a switch, instantly track everybody with a phone or a computer, know who they were, where they were, what they were doing with whom, and what they had ever done in the past.[11]

Snowden writes about a public speech that the Central Intelligence Agency's chief technology officer, Gus Hunt, gave to a tech group in 2013 that caused barely a ripple. Only *The Huffington Post* covered it. In the speech, Hunt said, "It is really very nearly within our grasp to be able to compute on all human-generated information." He added that after the CIA masters capturing that data, it intends to develop the capability of saving and analyzing it.[12]

Understand what this means: your private digital life belongs to the State, and always will. For the time being, we have laws and practices that prevent the government from using that information against individuals, unless it suspects they are involved in terrorism, criminal activity, or espionage. But over and over, dissidents told me that the law is not a reliable refuge: if the government is determined to take you out, it will manufacture a crime from the data it has captured, or otherwise deploy it to destroy your reputation.

Both the spread of the cult of social justice and the reach of surveillance capitalism into areas that the Orwellian tyrants of the communist bloc could only have aspired to have created an environment favorable to the emergence of soft totalitarianism. Under this Pink Police State scenario, powerful corporate and state actors will control populations by massaging them with digital velvet gloves, and by convincing them to surrender political liberties for security and convenience.

China: The Mark of the East

We don't have to imagine the dystopian merging of commerce and political authoritarianism in a total surveillance state. It already exists in the People's Republic of China. No doubt China's totalitarianism has become far more sophisticated than the crude Sino-Stalinism practiced by its first leader, Mao Zedong. Even in a worst-case scenario, it is hard to imagine the United States becoming as ruthless as the state that has incarcerated a million of its Muslim citizens in concentration camps in an effort to destroy their cultural identity.[13]

Nevertheless, China today proves that it is possible to have a wealthy, modern society and still be totalitarian. The techniques of social control that have become common in China could be adapted by America with relative ease. The fact that concentration camps in the American desert sound far-fetched should not keep us from understanding how much of China's surveillance system could be quickly made useful to corporate and government controllers here.

In the early 1980s, when Deng Xiaoping opened China to free-market reform, Western experts predicted that liberal democracy wouldn't be far behind. They believed that free markets and free minds were inseparable. All the West had to do was sit back and watch capitalism free the liberal democrat deep inside China's collective heart.

Forty years later, China has become spectacularly rich and powerful, creating in a single generation a robust, colorful consumer society from a mass population that had known poverty and struggle since time immemorial. The Chinese Communist Party, which worked this miracle, not only maintains a secure grip on political power but also is turning the nation of 1.4 billion souls into the most advanced totalitarian society the world has ever known.

Beijing's use of consumer data, biometric information, GPS tracking coordinates, facial recognition, DNA, and other forms of data harvesting has turned, and continues to turn, China into a beast never before seen worldwide, not even under Mao or Stalin. In China, the tools of surveillance capitalism are employed by the surveillance state to administer the so-called social credit system, which determines who is allowed to buy, sell, and travel, based on their social behavior.

"China is about to become something new: an AI-powered techno-totalitarian state," writes journalist John Lanchester. "The project aims to form not only a new kind of state but a new kind of human being, one who has fully internalized the demands of the state and the completeness of its surveillance and control. That internalization is the goal: agencies of the state will never need to intervene to correct the citizen's behavior, because the citizen has done it for them in advance."[14]

He is talking about Beijing's pioneering use of artificial intelligence and other forms of digital data gathering to create a state apparatus that not only monitors all citizens constantly but also can compel them to behave in ways the state demands without ever deploying the secret police or the threat of gulags (though those exist for the recalcitrant), and without suffering the widespread poverty that was the inevitable product of old-style communism.

The great majority of Chinese pay for consumer goods and services using smartphone apps or their faces, via facial recognition technology. These provide consumer convenience and security, making life easier for ordinary people. They also generate an enormous amount of personal data about each Chinese individual, all of which the government tracks.

The state has other uses for facial recognition technology. Television cameras are ubiquitous on Chinese streets, recording the daily comings and goings of the nation's people. Beijing's software is so advanced that it can easily check facial scans against the central security database. If a citizen enters an area forbidden to him—a church, say—or even if a person is merely walking in the opposite direction of a crowd, the system automatically records it and alerts the police.

In theory, police don't have to show up at the suspect's door to make him pay for his disobedience. China's social credit system automatically tracks the words and actions, online and off, of every Chinese citizen, and grants rewards or demerits based on obedience. A Chinese who does something socially positive—helping an elderly neighbor with a chore, or listening to a speech of leader Xi Jinping—receives points toward a higher social credit score. On the other hand, one who does something negative—letting his or her dog poop on the sidewalk, for example, or making a snarky comment on social media—suffers a social credit downgrade.

Because digital life, including commercial transactions, is automatically monitored, Chinese with high social credit ratings gain privileges. Those with lower scores find daily life harder. They aren't allowed to buy high-speed train tickets or take flights. Doors close to certain restaurants. Their children may not be allowed to go to college. They may lose their job and have a difficult time finding a new one. And a social credit scofflaw will find himself isolated, as the algorithmic system downgrades those who are connected to the offender.

The bottom line: a Chinese citizen cannot participate in the economy or society unless he has the mark of approval from Xi Jinping, the country's all-powerful leader. In a cashless society, the state has the power to bankrupt dissidents instantly by cutting off access to the internet. And in a society in which everyone is connected digitally, the state can make anyone an instant pariah when the algorithm turns them radioactive, even to their family.

The Chinese state is also utilizing totalitarian methods for ensuring the coming generations don't have the imaginative capacity to fight back.

In his 2019 book, *We Have Been Harmonized*—China's term for neutralizing citizens as a threat to the social and political order—veteran journalist Kai Strittmatter, who spent years in Beijing reporting for a German daily, reveals the techno-dystopia that modern China has become. He interviews a Chinese teacher who gives his name as "David," and who despairs of his country's future.

"People born in the 1980s and afterwards are hopelessly lost," David says. He continues:

> The brainwashing starts in nursery school. It was different for us. They called us a lost generation because schools and colleges were closed back then, and many of us were denied an education. But in reality, we were probably the lucky ones. We fell through the cracks. The brainwashing didn't get us. Mao was dead, and everyone was desperate for China to open up, for reform, freedom.[15]

The state's information-control apparatus has demolished the ability of young Chinese to learn facts about their nation's history in ways that contradict the Communist Party's narrative. The

1989 Tiananmen Square massacre, for example, has been memory-holed. This is something that we will almost certainly not have to endure in the West.

But the condition of the youth in consumerist China is more Huxley than Orwell. As the American media critic Neil Postman once said, Orwell feared a world in which people would be forbidden to read books. Huxley, by contrast, feared a world in which no one would have to ban books, because no one would want to read them in the first place. This, says David, is China today. Even though a great deal of information remains available to students, they don't care about it.

"My students say they haven't got time. They're distracted by a thousand other things," David tells Strittmatter. "And although I'm only ten years older than them, they don't understand me. They live in a completely different world. They've been perfectly manipulated by their education and the Party's propaganda: my students devote their lives to consumerism and ignore everything else. They ignore reality; it's been made easy for them."[16]

And so, a population that has been wholly propagandized by a totalitarian state, and demoralized by hedonistic consumerism, will hardly be in a position even to imagine opposition to its command-and-control strategies. And even if some dissidents did emerge, the government's total information system would quickly identify and "harmonize" them before they had the opportunity to act—*or even before they had the conscious thought of dissenting.*

Unnervingly, Strittmatter's reporting shows that Chinese officials are applying predictive software to its data culls to identify potential future leaders and possible enemies of the state before awareness of their potential rises to the individuals' minds.

Can It Happen Here?

Of course it can. The technological capability to implement such a system of discipline and control in the West already exists. The only barriers preventing it from being imposed are political resistance by unwilling majorities and constitutional resistance by the judiciary.

American culture is far more individualistic than Chinese culture, so that political resistance will almost certainly prevent Chinese-style hard totalitarianism from gaining a foothold here. But activating the broad reach of technology, especially the data-gathering technology that consumers have already accepted into their daily lives, and making it work to serve social justice goals is eminently feasible.

If democratic majorities come to believe that transferring social control to governmental and private institutional elites is necessary to guarantee virtue and safety, then it will happen. In the meantime, nothing is stopping immensely powerful corporations from bringing about soft totalitarianism within market democracy.

As of this writing, the global online payments transfer system PayPal refuses to let white supremacist groups use its services. It's hard to object to that, though First Amendment purists will feel some distress. But PayPal also stigmatizes some mainstream conservative groups. And as we have seen, some major banks now have policies that deny service to firearms manufacturers and sellers—this, even though guns are legal to make and to own under the Second Amendment. Note well that the government did not force these giant financial firms to adopt these policies. What is to stop private entities that control access to money and markets from redlining individuals, churches, and other organizations they deem to be bad social actors by denying access to commerce? China shows that it can be done, and how to do it.

Our changing personal habits accelerate the peril. The collapse of a commonly held belief in guarding online privacy removes the most important barrier to state control of private life. This is something that alarms those with experience under communism.

In Bratislava, the capital of Slovakia, photographer Timo Križka and his wife, Petra, are members of their country's first postcommunist generation. They were born around the time of the Velvet Revolution that overthrew the communist regime and the Velvet Divorce that peacefully separated the Czech Republic from Slovakia. Neither carries personal memories of communism, of course, but they did grow up in its immediate aftermath—and with parents and other adults who still had the habits developed under totalitarianism.

Petra took some of them with her to the United States when she went as an exchange student in 2005. This was not long after the 9/11 terrorist attack, when a heightened sense of security pervaded the country.

"I saw that people were willing to sacrifice a lot of their personal freedoms for the sake of national security," says Petra. "There was a lot of talk along the lines of, 'I don't care if they listen to my phone calls or read my emails or text messages, because I don't have anything bad to say.' So that was really strange for me, because I thought, this is something really personal. And it doesn't really matter if you do or don't have something bad to say. It's just my personal space."

How strange it was for a teenager to come from a culture just emerging from the reality of one careless word or indiscreet meeting having the potential to destroy a person's life, only to find herself living temporarily in one where everyone said whatever they wanted to, without a care in the world.

Should it not have felt liberating? Not to Petra, with her background in a society where privacy was precious. Her conflicting feelings highlight a philosophical and psychological dimension to the public-private divide over the meaning of living in truth. In his best-known novel, *The Unbearable Lightness of Being*, the Czech writer Milan Kundera contrasts the attitudes of two characters—Sabina, a Czech woman, and her Swiss lover, Franz—on the importance of personal privacy to authenticity.

For Franz, who had always lived in the West, to live in truth meant to live transparently, without any secrets. Yet for Sabina, a lifelong citizen of communist Czechoslovakia, living in truth was possible only within a private life.

"The moment someone keeps an eye on what we do, we involuntarily make allowances for that eye, and nothing we do is truthful," Kundera writes, speaking for Sabina. "Having a public, keeping a public in mind, means living in lies."[17]

Kundera's observations, emerging from his own experience of communism, are as relevant as ever. During the past decade or so, since the invention of the smartphone and social media, and the confessional culture they have created, we have gained a great deal of knowledge about how people—teenagers and young adults, mostly—create "Instagrammable" lives for themselves. That is, they say and do things, including sharing intensely personal information, to construct an image of a life that strikes their peers— whether they know them personally or not—as appealing, as desirable. They live for the approval of others, represented by Likes on Facebook, or other tokens of affirmation.

Psychologist Jean Twenge has tracked the astonishing rise of teenage depression and suicide among the first generation to come of age with smartphones and social media. She describes them "as being on the brink of the worst mental-health crisis in decades," and says that "much of this deterioration can be traced to their phones."[18]

Their deep unhappiness comes from the isolation they feel, despite being connected, thanks to smartphone-enabled social networking, to more people than any generation ever has. Smartphone culture has radically increased the social anxiety they experience, as information coming through their phones convinces sensitive teenagers—especially girls—that they are being left out of the more exciting lives others are having.

Of course most of their peers aren't having more vivid and intense lives; they are just better at curating their images online. Young people today are living in illusions, perhaps none greater than that they are part of a real social network. In fact, this technology and the culture that has emerged from it is reproducing the atomization and radical loneliness that totalitarian communist governments used to impose on their captive peoples to make them easier to control.

And having become habituated to sharing reams of personal data with marketers simply by moving through their daily lives online, these young people are making themselves highly vulnerable to manipulation by corporations and outside entities. To put it bluntly, we are being conditioned to accept a Westernized version of China's social credit system, which will enforce the tenets of the political cult of social justice. If this ever takes root here, there will be no place to hide. Christians and others who refuse to conform will be forced to pioneer a way to live in truth, despite it all.

This is why the testimonies of those who lived in truth under hard totalitarianism are so urgently needed.

Shelter from the Gathering Storm

In the West today, we are living under decadent, pre-totalitarian conditions. Social atomization, widespread loneliness, the rise of ideology, widespread loss of faith in institutions, and other factors leave society vulnerable to the totalitarian temptation to which both Russia and Germany succumbed in the previous century.

Furthermore, intellectual, cultural, academic, and corporate elites are under the sway of a left-wing political cult built around social justice. It is a militantly illiberal ideology that shares alarming commonalities with Bolshevism, including dividing humanity between the Good and the Evil. This pseudoreligion appears to meet a need for meaning and moral purpose in a post-Christian society and seeks to build a just society by demonizing, excluding, and even persecuting all who resist its harsh dogmas.

Finally, Big Business's embrace and promotion of progressive social values and the emergence of "surveillance capitalism"—the sales-directed mining of individual data gathered by electronic devices—is preparing the West to accept a version of China's social credit system. We are being conditioned to surrender privacy and political liberties for the sake of comfort, convenience, and an artificially imposed social harmony.

This is the brave new world of the twenty-first century. Christian dissidents will be unable to mount an effective resistance if their eyes aren't open to and focused on the nature and methods of social justice ideology and the ways in which data harvesting and manipulation can and will be used by woke capitalists and social justice ideologues in institutional authority to impose control.

It is coming, and it is coming fast. How should we resist it? That is the subject of the second half of this book.

PART TWO

How to Live in Truth

CHAPTER FIVE

Value Nothing More Than Truth

olzhenitsyn was not the only dissident to make "live not by lies" the core of anti-totalitarian resistance. Czech playwright and future postcommunist president Václav Havel's most famous injunction to would-be dissidents was to "live in truth." In his most important piece of political writing, which was secretly passed around by samizdat, Havel wrote about "the power of the powerless," which was the essay's title.

Havel knew that he was addressing a nation that had no way to rise up against the might of the Czechoslovak police state. But he also knew something most of them did not: they were not entirely powerless.

Consider, he said, the case of the greengrocer who posts a sign in his shop bearing the well-known slogan from the Communist Manifesto, "Workers of the world, unite!" He doesn't believe in it. He hangs it in his shop as a signal of his own conformity. He just wants to be left alone. His action is not meaningless though: the greengrocer's act not only confirms that this is what is expected of one in a communist society but also perpetuates the belief that this is what it means to be a good citizen.

Havel goes on:

> Let us now imagine that one day something in our green-grocer snaps and he stops putting up the slogans merely to ingratiate himself. He stops voting in elections he knows are a farce. He begins to say what he really thinks at po-litical meetings. And he even finds the strength in himself to express solidarity with those whom his conscience com-mands him to support. In this revolt the greengrocer steps out of living within the lie. He rejects the ritual and breaks the rules of the game. He discovers once more his sup-pressed identity and dignity. He gives his freedom a con-crete significance. His revolt is an attempt to live within the truth.[1]

This costs him. He loses his shop, his salary is cut, and he won't be able to travel abroad. Maybe his children won't be able to get into college. People persecute him and those around him—not nec-essarily because they oppose his stance but because they know that this is what they have to do to keep the authorities off their backs.

The poor little greengrocer, who testifies to the truth by refus-ing to mouth a lie, suffers. But there is a deeper meaning to his gesture.

> By breaking the rules of the game, he has disrupted the game as such. He has exposed it as a mere game. He has shattered the world of appearances, the fundamental pillar

of the system. He has upset the power structure by tearing apart what holds it together. He has demonstrated that living a lie is living a lie. He has broken through the exalted facade of the system and exposed the real, base foundations of power. He has said that the emperor is naked. And because the emperor is in fact naked, something extremely dangerous has happened: by his action, the greengrocer has addressed the world. He has enabled everyone to peer behind the curtain. He has shown everyone that it is possible to live within the truth. Living within the lie can constitute the system only if it is universal. The principle must embrace and permeate everything. There are no terms whatsoever on which it can co-exist with living within the truth, and therefore everyone who steps out of line denies it in principle and threatens it in its entirety.[2]

A Russian Orthodox mystic of the nineteenth century, Saint Seraphim of Sarov, once said, "Acquire the Holy Spirit, and thousands around you will be saved." In that sense, what the greengrocer has done is a small act of rebellion that may act as the spark of a revolution that saves liberty and humanity.

A person who lives only for his own comfort and survival and who is willing to live within a lie to protect that, is, says Havel, "a demoralized person.

"The system depends on this demoralization, deepens it, is in fact a projection of it into society," he writes. "Living within the truth, as humanity's revolt against an enforced position, is, on the contrary, an attempt to regain control over one's own sense of responsibility."[3]

Václav Havel published that essay in 1978. A year later, the communist government returned the troublemaking writer to prison. Ten years later, Havel led a revolution that peacefully toppled the regime and became the first president of a free Czechoslovakia.

In time, a mere writer willing to suffer for truth took power from totalitarian zealots who marshaled an entire state in the service of lies. In the happy fate of Havel, we see the truth of an old Russian proverb, beloved by Solzhenitsyn: "One word of truth outweighs the whole world."

It is up to us today to take up this challenge, to live not by lies and to speak the truth that defeats evil. How do we do this in a society built on lies? By accepting a life outside the mainstream, courageously defending the truth, and being willing to endure the consequences. These challenges are daunting, but we are blessed with examples from saints who've gone before.

Choose a Life Apart from the Crowd

I am sitting at the luncheon table of Father Kirill Kaleda inside the toasty warm wooden building that serves as his office. A late autumn snow fell outside, over the Butovo Firing Range, the field in the forested far southern reaches of Moscow where, in a fourteen-month period between 1937 and 1938, agents of the NKVD (secret police) executed about twenty-one thousand political prisoners—among them, one thousand priests and bishops. Thanks to the advocacy work of Father Kirill, the field is now a national monument to the dead. On the day I visited, Russian citizens gathered outside in the cold to solemnly read aloud the names of each murdered countryman to honor their memories and to remember what Soviet totalitarianism had done to them.

"How does an honest man live under totalitarianism?" I ask the priest, a broad-shouldered man with a thick brown beard and piercing eyes.

"With difficulty," he says, laughing. "Of course it's difficult, but thanks be to God, there were people who were doing their best to build their lives in such a way that they could live in truth. People understood that if that was going to be a priority to live in truth, then they were going to have to limit themselves in other ways— the progress of their careers, for example. But they made a choice, and resolved to live by it."

Father Kirill grew up in an Orthodox Christian family with six children. None joined the Communist Youth League, the Komsomol.

"When I was a teenager, I wanted to study history," he says. "My father explained to me that in the Soviet world, trying to be involved with history and not be involved with Soviet ideology is impossible. So I became a geologist. Lots of anti-Bolshevik families sent their kids to study the natural sciences to avoid contamination with the ideology as much as possible."

Refusing to join the Komsomol meant that he would not be permitted to travel abroad. Once, as a student, Father Kirill was offered an exciting ship voyage from Vladivostok, on the Soviet east coast, down to Australia, Singapore, up through the Suez Canal, and back home through the Black Sea. It was a dream come true—but he would have to be a Komsomol member to take the trip. Rather than violate his conscience, Kirill declined, and proposed a Komsomol friend in his place. The sea journey changed his friend's life.

"To this day, that friend does a lot of traveling across seas and oceans," the priest remembers. He, by contrast, tends this garden of sacred memory, and pastors the new church built nearby in honor of the martyrs of the Soviet yoke.

Two days later, I sat in a café in the heart of Moscow listening to Yuri Sipko, a retired Baptist pastor. In his village classroom in the 1950s in Siberia, Sipko and his classmates were given a badge with a portrait of Lenin. At age eleven, the children were given the red scarf of the Young Pioneers, a kind of Boy Scouts and Girl Scouts for communist youth. Teachers drilled the children in the slogan of the Pioneers: "Be ready. Always be ready."

"I didn't wear the pin with Lenin's face, nor did I wear the red scarf. I was a Baptist. I wasn't going to do that," recalls Sipko. "I was the only one in my class. They went after my teachers. They wanted to know what they were doing wrong that they had a boy in their class who wasn't a Pioneer. They pressured the director of the school too. They were forced to pressure me to save themselves."

To be a Baptist in Soviet Russia was to know that you were a permanent outsider. They endured it because they knew that truth was embodied in Jesus Christ, and that to live apart from him would mean living a lie. For the Baptists, to compromise with lies for the sake of a peaceful life is to bend at the knee to death.

"When I think about the past, and how our brothers were sent to prison and never returned, I'm sure that this is the kind of certainty they had," says the old pastor. "They lost any kind of status. They were mocked and ridiculed in society. Sometimes they even lost their children. Just because they were Baptists, the state was willing to take away their kids and send them to orphanages. These believers were unable to find jobs. Their children were not able to enter universities. And still, they believed."

The Baptists stood alone, but stand they did. If you have been discipled in a faith that takes seriously the Apostle Paul's words that to suffer for Christ is gain and are prepared, as the Orthodox Kaleda family was, to live with reduced expectations of worldly success, it becomes easier to stand for the truth.

Reject Doublethink and Fight for Free Speech

Vladimir Grygorenko and Olga Rusanova, husband and wife, immigrated from Ukraine to the United States in the year 2000 and now live in Texas. They tell me that if you grow up in a culture of lies, as they did, you don't know that life could be any other way.

"The general culture taught you doublethink," says Grygorenko. "That was normal life."

"In high school and middle school, we had to write essays, like normal school kids do," says Rusanova. "But you never could write what you think about the subject. Never, ever. The subject could be interesting, but you never can say what you really think. You have to find some way to relate it to the communist point of view."

When a people grow accustomed to living in lies, shunning taboo writers, and conforming to the official story, it deforms their way of thinking, says Grygorenko—and that is very difficult to overcome. He is concerned by polls showing that Americans' support for the First Amendment—which guarantees the constitutional right to free expression—is waning, especially among younger Americans, who are increasingly intolerant of dissenting opinion. Grygorenko sees this as a sign that society prefers the false peace of conformity to the tensions of liberty. To grow indifferent, even hostile, to free speech is suicidal for a free people.

"In this country, what we need to do is protect free speech," says Grygorenko, who became a proud American citizen in 2019. "The First Amendment is important. For us, the Soviet constitution had no meaning. Everybody knew these were just words that had no relation to real life. In this country, the Constitution *is* meaningful. We have an independent judiciary. We have to protect it. We don't need to invent anything new—we just need to have the courage to protect what we have."

Defending the right to speak and write freely, even when it costs you something, is the duty of every free person. So says Mária Wittner, a hero of the 1956 Hungarian uprising against Soviet occupation. A communist court sentenced Wittner, then only twenty, to death, though this was later commuted to life imprisonment.

"Once I said to one of the guards in prison, 'You are lying.' For that alone, I was taken to trial again," remembers the feisty Wittner. "The state prosecutor said to me, 'Wittner, why did you accuse the guard of being a liar? Why didn't you just say, 'You're not telling the truth'? I said, 'It matters that we speak plainly.'"

For her insolence, Wittner was sent back to prison with extra punishments. She had to sleep on a wooden bed with no mattress and was given reduced rations. By the time her sentence was commuted and she was released, Wittner weighed scarcely one hundred pounds. Nevertheless, she insists that a broken body is a price worth paying for a strong and undefiled spirit.

"We live in a world of lies, whether we want it or not. That's just the case. But you shouldn't accommodate to it," she tells me as I sit at her table in suburban Budapest. "You will be surrounded by lies—you don't have a choice. Don't assimilate to it. It's an individual decision for each person. If you want to live in fear, or if you want to live in the freedom of the soul. If your soul is free, then your thoughts are free, and then your words are going to be free."

Under hard totalitarianism, dissenters like Wittner paid a hard price for their freedom, but the terms of the bargain were clear. Under soft totalitarianism, it is more difficult to see the costs of compromising your conscience, but as Mária Wittner insists, you can't escape the decisions. You have to live in a world of lies, but it's your choice as to whether that world lives in you.

Cherish Truth-Telling but Be Prudent

While it is imperative to fight assimilation to lies, combating the lies doesn't mean refusing all compromise. Ordinary life, in every society, requires assessing which fights are worth having in a given context. Though one must guard against rationalization, prudence is not the same thing as cowardice.

As a Hungarian Boy Scout, Tamás Sályi's father had been linked to a typewriter on which someone composed anti-Soviet propaganda. The year was 1946, and the Red Army occupied Hungary. All the Scouts connected to the typewriter suffered punishment—death, exile, or in the case of the elder Sályi, internment without charge in a prison camp.

In 1963, when Tamás was only seven years old, he came home from school and told his father how the Soviet Army had liberated their nation.

"He said, 'Boy, sit down,'" Tamás remembers. "He began to tell me stories about the '56 uprising and the Soviet invasion. He told me the truth, and when he finished, he warned me never to talk about that at school."

Tamás glances down at the floor of his Budapest living room.

"We have so many problems today because fathers never talked to their sons as my father did to me in 1963."

Tamás Sályi's point is that parents were so afraid that their children would be punished for inadvertently telling the truth that they chose not to tell them the truth at all about their country's history and regime. Sályi's father, though he knew from personal experience how vicious the communists were, believed that his son deserved the truth—but should also be taught how to handle himself with it.

Judit Pastor, Tamás's wife and a literature teacher at a Catholic university, also watched her father suffer from persecution—though his fate was much crueler. He was sacked as a military journalist for refusing to swear a loyalty oath to the government installed by the Soviets following the 1956 invasion.

Then, in 1968, outraged by the persecution of ethnic Hungarians by the communist government in neighboring Romania, Judit's father went to a trade fair in Budapest, ripped down a poster of dictator Nicolae Ceaușescu at Romania's exhibit, and stomped on it. For that, he received eighteen months in jail.

It shattered him.

"Based on the Soviet method, it was common practice to label political prisoners mentally ill and give them treatment," says Judit. "He got fifty electroshocks. He suffered a heart attack as a result of the electroshock, but it was never treated. His wasn't an uncommon case."

When Judit's father was released, he was a shell of himself. He was diagnosed as schizophrenic, put on a medical pension, and reduced to living on the margins. Judit's mother divorced him after a while. No one in the family spoke of it. Ever.

The family's code of silence about what was done to Judit's father was an excruciating burden for her.

Today, though, she speaks openly about what communism did to her dad, especially to the university students she teaches. She is also campaigning to have his name posthumously cleared. This too is a matter of telling the truth.

"It has been a constant struggle for me to make people acknowledge what happened to my father. People don't want to listen. They don't want to know about that," she says. "Whether you live under oppression or not, it's an ongoing and constant struggle for truth."

Pastor takes comfort that one of her sons has taken up the cause for which his grandfather essentially gave his life: the plight of persecuted ethnic Hungarians. Yet this woman who lived through the destruction of her family over her father's recklessly brave decision to take a stand for the truth says that there is a lot to be said for passive opposition.

"Sometimes silence is an act of resistance. Not just standing up for the truth by communicating loudly—keeping silent when you aren't expected to be silent. That, too, is telling the truth."

See, Judge, Act

The dictatorship of thought and word under construction by progressives is a regime based on lies and propaganda. Most conservatives, Christian and not, recognize that to some degree, but too few see the deeper ramifications of accepting these lies. "Political correctness" is an annoyance; these lies corrupt one's ability to think clearly about reality.

Once you perceive how the system runs on lies, stand as firmly as you can on what you know to be true and real when confronted by those lies. Refuse to let the media and institutions propagandize your children. Teach them how to identify lies and to refuse them. Do your best not be party to the lie—not for the sake of professional advantage, personal status, or any other reason. Sometimes you will have to act openly to confront the lie directly. Other times you will fight it by remaining silent and withholding the approval authorities request. You might have to raise your voice to defend someone who is being slandered by propagandists.

Judging when and how to confront the lie depends on individual circumstances, of course. As Father Kaleda says, the faith does not require one to actively seek opportunities for martyrdom. Most of us will be forced by circumstances and responsibilities to our families to be something less than a Solzhenitsyn. That doesn't necessarily make us cowards.

But take care not to let reasoning prudentially turn into rationalization. That is the basis of *ketman*—and to surrender to that kind of self-defense will, over time, destroy your soul. Your consent to the system's lies might buy you safety, but at an unbearable cost. If you cannot imagine *any* situation in which you would act like Havel's fictional greengrocer, and live in truth no matter the cost or consequence, then cowardice has a greater claim on your conscience than you know.

A society's values are carried in the stories it chooses to tell about itself and in the people it wishes to honor. Havel's greengrocer is a myth that teaches a lesson about the importance of bearing witness to the truth, no matter what; the real-life stories of national heroes like Mária Wittner, and lesser-known resisters like Pastor Yuri Sipko and Father Kirill Kaleda, tell the same story. All of these stories are also important to tell and retell as a guide to others, including those generations as yet unborn. Totalitarians, both soft and hard, know this, which is why they exert such effort to control the common narrative.

CHAPTER SIX

Cultivate Cultural Memory

Who controls the past, controls the future:
who controls the present controls the past.

THE PARTY SLOGAN,
NINETEEN EIGHTY-FOUR

Recently, a bright-eyed and cheerful twenty-six-year-old California woman told me that she thinks of herself as a communist. "It's just so beautiful, this dream of everybody being equal," she gushed. When she asked me what I was working on, I told her about the struggles of Alexander Ogorodnikov, a Christian dissident imprisoned and tortured by the Soviets, whom I had recently interviewed in Moscow. She fell silent.

"Don't you know about the gulag?" I asked, naively.

Of course she didn't. Nobody ever told her. We, her parents and grandparents, have failed her generation. And if she develops no curiosity about the past, she will fail herself.

She's not alone. Every year, the Victims of Communism Memorial Foundation, a nonprofit educational and research organization established by the US Congress, carries out a survey of Americans to determine their attitudes toward communism, socialism, and Marxism in general. In 2019, the survey found that a startling number of Americans of the post–Cold War generations have favorable views of left-wing radicalism, and only 57 percent of millennials believe that the Declaration of Independence offers a better guarantee of "freedom and equality" than the Communist Manifesto. The political religion that murdered tens of millions, imprisoned and tortured countless more, and immiserated the lives of half of humanity in its time, and the defeat of which required agonizing struggle by allies across borders, oceans, political parties, and generations—this hateful ideology is romanticized by ignorant young people.[1]

Writing in the *The Harvard Crimson* in 2017, undergraduate Laura Nicolae, whose parents endured the horrors of Romanian communism, spoke out against the falsification of history that her fellow Ivy Leaguers receive, both in class and in the trendy Marxism of intellectual student culture.

"Depictions of communism on campus paint the ideology as revolutionary or idealistic, overlooking its authoritarian violence," she writes. "Instead of deepening our understanding of the world, the college experience teaches us to reduce one of the most destructive ideologies in human history to a one-dimensional, sanitized narrative."[2]

Forgetting the atrocities of communism is bad enough. What is even more dangerous is the habit of forgetting one's past. The Czech novelist Milan Kundera drily observes that nobody today will defend gulags, but the world remains full of suckers for the false utopian promises that bring gulags into existence.

"Not to know what happened before you were born is to remain a child forever," said Cicero. This, explains Kundera, is why communists placed such emphasis on conquering the minds and hearts of young people. In his novel *The Book of Laughter and Forgetting*, Kundera recalls a speech that Czech president Gustáv Husák gave to a group of Young Pioneers, urging them to keep pressing forward to the Marxist paradise of peace, justice, and equality.

> "Children, never look back," [Kundera's character Husák] cried, and what he meant was that we must never allow the future to collapse under the burden of memory.[3]

A collective loss of historical memory—not just memory of communism but memory of our shared cultural past—within the West is bound to have a devastating effect on our future. It's not that forgetting the evils of communism means we are in danger of re-creating precisely that form of totalitarianism. It's that the act of forgetting itself makes us vulnerable to totalitarianism in general.

Put another way, we not only have to remember totalitarianism to build a resistance to it; we have to remember how to remember, period.

Why Memory Matters

Everything about modern society is designed to make memory—historical, social, and cultural—hard to cultivate. Christians must understand this not only to resist soft totalitarianism but also to transmit the faith to the coming generations.

In his 1989 book, *How Societies Remember*, the late British social anthropologist Paul Connerton explains that there are different kinds of memory. Historical memory is an objective recollection of past events. Social memory is what a people choose to remember—that is, deciding collectively which facts about past events it believes to be important. Cultural memory constitutes the stories, events, people, and other phenomena that a society chooses to remember as the building blocks of its collective identity. A nation's gods, its heroes, its villains, its landmarks, its art, its music, its holidays—all these things are part of its cultural memory.

Connerton says that "participants in any social order must presuppose a shared memory."[4] Memory of the past conditions how they experience the present—that is, how they grasp its meaning, how they are to understand it, and what they are supposed to do in it.

No culture, and no person, can remember everything. A culture's memory is the result of its collective sifting of facts to produce a story—a story that society tells itself to remember who it is. Without collective memory, you have no culture, and without a culture, you have no identity.

The more totalitarian a regime's nature, the more it will try to force people to forget their cultural memories. In *Nineteen Eighty-Four*, the role of Winston Smith within the Ministry of Information is to erase all newspaper records of past events to reflect the current political priorities of the Party. This, said the ex-communist Polish intellectual Leszek Kołakowski, reflects "the great ambition of totalitarianism—the total possession and control of human memory."

"Let us consider what happens when the ideal has been effectively achieved," says Kołakowski. "People remember only what they are taught to remember today and the content of their memory changes overnight, if needed."[5]

We know from the history of communist totalitarianism how this can be achieved through a total state monopoly on information, including ideological control of education and media. Laura Nicolae's experience at Harvard, where the next generation of American and global elites are trained, suggests how this can be accomplished even in free countries: by teaching those who aspire to leadership positions what it is important for them to remember, and what does not matter.

It is not news to Western conservatives that ideologues in power, both in classrooms and newsrooms, manipulate collective memory to capture the future. What is much less present in the consciousness of modern people, as Connerton avers, is how the liberal democratic, capitalist way of life unintentionally does the same thing.

The essence of modernity is to deny that there are any transcendent stories, structures, habits, or beliefs to which individuals must submit and that should bind our conduct. To be modern is to be free to choose. *What* is chosen does not matter; the meaning is in the choice itself. There is no sacred order, no other world, no fixed virtues and permanent truths. There is only here and now and the eternal flame of human desire. *Volo ergo sum*—I want, therefore I am.

Cultural memories function to legitimize the present social order, says Connerton. This is why people in "subordinate groups"—that is, social minorities—have such a hard time holding on to their cultural memories. To keep the memories alive means fighting against the dominant order.

Communism had a particular ideological vision that required it to destroy traditions, including traditional Christianity. Nothing outside the communist order could be allowed to exist. Similarly, in contemporary capitalism, cultural memory is subordinate to the logic of the free market, whose mechanisms respond to the liberation of individual desire. Christians today find it difficult to pass on the faith to the young in large part because all of us have become habituated to a way of life in which there are few if any shared beliefs and customs that transcend individualism. This is what Cardinal Joseph Ratzinger meant, on the eve of his election as Pope Benedict XVI, when he condemned "the dictatorship of relativism."[6]

To those who want to keep cultural memory alive, Connerton warns that it is not enough to pass on historical information to the young. The truths carried by tradition must be lived out subjectively. That is, they must not only be studied but also embodied in shared social practices—words, certainly, but more important, deeds. Communities must have "living models"[7] of men and women who enact these truths in their daily lives. Nothing else works.

Tamás Sályi, the Budapest teacher, says that Hungarians survived German occupation and a Soviet puppet regime, but thirty years of freedom has destroyed more cultural memory than the previous eras. "What neither Nazism or Communism could do, victorious liberal capitalism has done," he muses.

The idea that the past and its traditions, including religion, is an intolerable burden on individual liberty has been poison for Hungarians, he believes. About progressives today, Sályi says, "I think they really believe that if they erase all memory of the past, and turn everyone into newborn babies, then they can write whatever they want on that blank slate. If you think about it, it's not so easy to manipulate people who know who they are, rooted in tradition."

True. This is why Hannah Arendt described the totalitarian personality as "the completely isolated human being." A person cut off from history is a person who is almost powerless against power.

Communism was a massive use of lethal state power to destroy memory. Back in the United States, Olga Rusanova, a naturalized American who grew up in Siberia, says, "In the Soviet Union, they killed all the people who could remember history." This made it easier for them to create false history to serve the regime's needs.

Yes, in the late Soviet period, most people had ceased to believe the communist line. But that doesn't mean that they knew what was true. As historian Orlando Figes says of those who came of age after the 1917 Bolshevik Revolution, "for anyone below the age of thirty, who had only ever known the Soviet world or had inherited no other values from his family, it was almost impossible to step outside the propaganda system and question its political principles."[8]

Create Small Fortresses of Memory

Figes's observation points to one source of resistance: the family and the cultural memories it passes on. Paul Connerton highlights another: religion.

Both come up in my conversation with Paweł Skibiński, one of Poland's leading historians, and the head of Warsaw's Museum of John Paul II Collection. We are talking about what Karol Wojtyła, the great anti-communist pope, has to teach us about resisting the new soft totalitarianism.

When the Nazis invaded Poland, they knew they could subdue the country by superior force of arms. But Hitler's plan for Poland was to destroy the Poles as a people. To do that, the Nazis needed to destroy the two things that gave the Polish their identity: their shared Catholic faith and their sense of themselves as a nation.

Before he entered seminary in 1943, Wojtyła was an actor in Krakow. He and his theatrical comrades knew that the survival of the Polish nation depended on keeping alive its cultural memory in the face of forced forgetting. They wrote and performed plays—Wojtyła himself authored three of them—about Polish national history, and Catholic Christianity. They performed these plays in secret for clandestine audiences. Had the Gestapo discovered the truth, the players and their audiences would have been sent to prison camps or shot.

Not every member of the anti-totalitarian resistance carries a rifle. Rifles would have been mostly useless against the German army. The persistence of cultural memory was the greatest weapon the Poles had to resist Nazi totalitarianism, and the Soviet kind, which seized the nation in the aftermath of Germany's defeat.

In Poland, Skibiński explains, the only long-lasting social institutions that existed were the church and the family. In the twentieth century, the twin totalitarianisms tried to capture and destroy the Polish Catholic Church. Communism attempted to break apart the family by maintaining a monopoly on education and teaching young people to be dependent on the state. It also sought to lure the young away from the church by convincing them that the state would be the guarantors of their sexual freedom.

"The thing is, now such tendencies come from the West, which we have always looked up to, and regarded as a safe place," he says. "But now many Poles start to develop the awareness that the West is no longer safe for us.

"What we see now is an attempt to destroy the last surviving communities: the family, the church, and the nation. This is one connection between liberalism and communist theory."

Skibiński focuses on language as a preserver of cultural memory. We know that communists forbade people to talk about history in unapproved ways. This is a tactic today's progressives use as well, especially within universities.

What is harder for contemporary people to appreciate is how we are repeating the Marxist habit of falsifying language, hollowing out familiar words and replacing them with a new, highly ideological meaning. Propaganda not only changes the way we think about politics and contemporary life but it also conditions what a culture judges worth remembering.

I mention the way liberals today deploy neutral-sounding, or even positive, words like *dialogue* and *tolerance* to disarm and ultimately defeat unaware conservatives. And they imbue other words and phrases—*hierarchy*, for example, or *traditional family*—with negative connotations.

Recalling life under communism, the professor continues, "The people who lived only within such a linguistic sphere, who didn't know any other way to speak, they could really start believing in this way of using of words. If a word carries with it negative baggage, it becomes impossible to have a discussion about the phenomenon."

Teaching current generations of college students who grew up in the postcommunist era is challenging because they do not have a natural immunity to the ideological abuse of language. "For me, it's obvious. I remember this false use of language. But for our students, it's impossible to understand."

How did people keep hold of reality under communist conditions? How do they know not only what to remember but how to remember it? The answer was to create distinct small communities—especially families and religious fellowships—in which it was possible both to speak truthfully and to embody truth.

"They had social spaces where the real meaning of words was preserved," he says. "For me, it's less important to argue with such a view of the world"—progressivism, he means—"than to describe reality as it is. For example, our task is to show people what a normal, monogamous family looks like."

To paraphrase Orwell in *Nineteen Eighty-Four*, it is not by winning an argument but by keeping yourself grounded in reality that you carry on the human heritage.

Make the Parallel Polis into Sanctuary Cities

Families and religious fellowships were places of retreat. So were underground educational seminars. These things were part of a communal concept that one prominent dissident called the "parallel polis."

Under communism, Czech mathematician and human rights activist Václav Benda knew that there was no place in the public square for noncommunists to have a say over how the country was to be governed. Communists held a monopoly on politics, on the media, and on the institutions of Czech life. But Benda refused to accept that dissenters had no choice but to resign themselves to surrender.

He came up with the idea of a *parallel polis*—an alternative set of social structures within which social and intellectual life could be lived outside of official approval. The parallel polis was a grassroots attempt to fight back against totalitarianism, which mandated, in Benda's words, "the abandonment of reason and learning [and] the loss of traditions and memory."[9]

"Totalitarian power has extended the sphere of politics to include everything, even the faith, the thinking and the conscience of the individual," he writes. "The first responsibility of a Christian and a human being is therefore to oppose such an inappropriate demand of the political sphere, *ergo* to resist totalitarian power."

A key institution of the parallel polis was the seminar held in private homes. In these events, scholars would lecture on forbidden subjects—history, literature, and other cultural topics necessary to maintaining cultural memory. Benda's parallel polis was not merely a federation of discussion groups biding their time by talking about intellectual and artistic topics. Rather, its driving purpose was first, cultural preservation in the face of annihilation, and by doing so, the cultivation of the seeds of renewal.

Sir Roger Scruton was one of the few Western academics who participated in these seminars, and who even helped establish an underground university that granted degrees in secret. Other prominent Western intellectuals, including philosopher Charles Taylor and literary critic Jacques Derrida, joined the fight. Derrida, like Scruton, was once detained by the Czech secret police and declared to be an "undesirable person."

When he and his British academic colleagues began to visit communist Czechoslovakia in the late 1970s, Scruton tells me, they were astonished to discover that the Czechs "were determined to cling to their cultural inheritance because they thought that it contained the truth, not just about their history, but the truth about their soul, about what they fundamentally are. That was the thing that the communists couldn't take away."

Scruton and his team discovered that the Czech students were starving for knowledge, and not just theoretical knowledge. They wanted to learn so they could know how to live, especially under a dictatorship of lies. Along those lines, in *Notes from Underground*, his 2014 novel set in Czechoslovakia of the 1980s, Scruton's protagonist, a young man named Jan, finds his way into Prague dissident circles. His guide tells him what to expect:

> And he added that there would be special seminars from time to time, with visitors from the West, who would inform us of the latest scholarship, and help us to remember. "To remember what?" I asked. He looked at me long and hard. "To remember what we are."[10]

These seminars forged what Scruton, quoting Czech dissident Jan Patočka, described as "the solidarity of the shattered." They were an act of responsibility by the old—those who still had their memories of what was real—toward the young. The formal institutions of Czech life—universities first among them—could no longer be trusted to tell the truth and to transmit the cultural memories that told Czechs who they were. But the task had to be done, or as Milan Hübl said, the Czech people would disappear.

Bear Communal Witness to Future Generations

There is a field in the far southern reaches of Moscow called the Butovo Firing Range. Under Soviet rule, it belonged to the secret police, the NKVD, who used it for target practice. During the height of Stalin's Great Terror, in a fourteen-month period between 1937 and 1938, the NKVD killed 20,761 political prisoners in that field—most of them with a shot to the back of the head—and buried them there.

In 1995, four years after the collapse of the Soviet Union, the Russian Orthodox Church took possession of the Butovo field. Today, there is a tiny wooden chapel on the site and a large stone church nearby dedicated to the martyrs of the Soviet period. The field itself is a national memorial site in which a monument to the dead stands, the name of each carved onto a granite wall, with the date of his or her death.

On October 30, all Russia observes a national Day of Remembrance for victims of political violence. Here at Butovo field, Russians gather on the site to read the names of the murdered aloud. There I stand in the clearing surrounded by bare trees, wet snow falling on a somber crowd of heavily bundled Russians, observing this ritual of collective memory. After a while, my translator Matthew Casserly and I wander over to an exhibit on the site's periphery, where the story of Butovo field is told in Russian.

An old man wearing a flat cap overhears Matthew translating the Russian for me. He sidles over, introduces himself as Vladimir Alexandrovich, and asks what brings us to Butovo today. Matthew tells him that his American friend is here to learn about the communist era, because émigrés in the West see signs of its potential rebirth there.

Like what? asks Vladimir Alexandrovich. I tell him about people afraid of losing their jobs for dissenting from left-wing ideology.

"Losing jobs?" he says. "That's a bad sign. It can happen again, you know. Young people don't know this, and they don't want to know. History always repeats, one way or the other."

Matthew and I make our way over to the large wooden cabin that serves as the national memorial's office. Father Kirill Kaleda, whom you met earlier in this story, is the Russian Orthodox priest who oversees the shrine and the nearby church. Father Kirill is the man chiefly responsible for convincing the Russian state to set aside this bloodsoaked land as a place of remembrance—and, he hopes, repentance. He had spent the morning telling students at a nearby school about the history of the site.

As we prepare to sit down with Father Kirill around a kitchen table laden with herring, salads, cheeses, breads, and other delicious things for the day's pilgrims to eat, I tell the priest about what we have just heard from the old man: Butovo could happen again.

"Unfortunately, he's right," says the priest. "I could clearly see that young people I was talking to today know nothing about what happened here. When I started talking about very simple things, I could see they knew nothing."

These are young people who live close enough to the Butovo field to have heard the sound of the gunshots back in the Great Terror. The signs of the mass murder here have been preserved in granite for all to see. Yet if not for Father Kirill visiting their classrooms to tell this story, the great-grandchildren of the murdered generation would have minds untroubled by the memory of mass murder.

Father Kirill was thirty-three years old when the Soviet Union fell. This man who grew up in the culture of official lies, and who has given his life to maintaining the historical memory of Bolshevik crimes, emphasizes that propaganda did not die with the USSR.

"Despite the fact that there's so much information available, we see that so much propaganda is also available. Think of what's happening now with Ukraine," he says, referring to the armed conflict between Russian-backed separatists and the Kiev government.

"We have seen the way TV changed us Russians from thinking of them as our family to being our enemies," he says. "The same methods from the communist era are being used. People today have a responsibility to search out more information than what they are offered on TV, and to know how to look critically on what they're reading and seeing. That's what is different now than before."

His point was that the cultural memories Russians have of closeness with Ukrainians are being erased thanks to propaganda.

As we talk, a woman comes in from the cold and takes a seat at the table. She is Marina Nikonovna Suslova, the Moscow city official in charge of rehabilitating the names of political prisoners. She is passionate about the work of preserving the memory of what communism did to the oppressed. She grows visibly impatient with the priest's modesty in our interview and leaps into the conversation.

"This memorial would not exist if not for your faith!" she exclaims to the priest. Then she turns to me.

"Father Kirill is a historical figure in Russia, and he will remain one, because it was his faith that allowed him to create this memorial complex," she says. "It was inspired by his faith, specifically.

This historical complex not only gives a different view of history, it gives a different feel of history. And it's telling a truth that needs to be told."

It is—and it is telling that truth not only in words but also embodying it in place and ritual.

See, Judge, Act

Memory, historical and otherwise, is a weapon of cultural self-defense. History is not just what is written in textbooks. History is in the stories we tell ourselves about who we were and who we are. History is embedded in the language we use, the things we make, and the rituals we observe. History is culture—and so is Christianity. To be indifferent or even hostile to tradition is to surrender to those in power who want to legitimate a new social and political order. To perceive the critical importance of memory and the role culture plays in preserving and transmitting it is critically important for Christianity's survival.

We have to tell our stories—in literature, film, theater, and other media—but we must also manifest cultural memory in communal deeds—in mourning and in celebration, in solemn remembrance and festal joy. The crowd of Russians who stood at Butovo field in the cold, wet autumn weather to read out the names of the murdered—theirs was a poignant act of cultural memory. So were the theatrical performances of Wojtyła and his troupe behind closed doors in occupied Poland. Seminars on literature, history, philosophy, and theology that dissidents held in their apartments to help one other remember who they were—these are things Christians in our post-Christian societies should revive. Classical Christian schooling, both in institutions and in home settings, is a great way to revive and preserve cultural memory. Less academically, we can celebrate festivals, make pilgrimages, observe holy-day practices, pray litanies, perform concerts, hold dances, learn and teach traditional cooking—any kind of collective deed that connects the community with its shared sacred and secular history in a living way is an act of resistance to an ethos that says the past doesn't matter.

Less formal, everyday acts within the home are more powerful than you might think. The way Christians talk about God and weave the stories of the Bible and church history into the fabric of domestic life is of immense significance, precisely because these things are so ordinary. This is training children and parents alike in cultural memory. The language Christians use—the words, the metaphors—matters, as does the way we pray together and the symbols we employ to embody and transmit meaning across the generations. We may not be able to communicate that meaning to a world gone insane, but as Orwell knew, simply by staying sane when everyone else is mad, we may hope to convey the human heritage.

CHAPTER SEVEN

Families Are Resistance Cells

F amily is where we first learn to love others. If we are lucky, it is also where we first learn how to live in truth.

The loosening of family ties and of traditional commitments to marriage has left Americans without the kind of refuge in the home that anti-communist dissidents had. US Christians, alas, are not especially different from unbelievers.

There is a strong model of anti-totalitarian resistance based in the Christian family: the Benda clan of Prague. The Bendas are a large Catholic family who suffered greatly in 1979 when the Czechoslovak state sentenced their patriarch, Václav, to four years in prison for his activities fighting for human rights.

Václav Benda and his wife, Kamila, both academics, were among the only believing Christians working at the topmost level of the Czech dissident movement. It wasn't easy living as Christians in Prague back then, and not only because of the atheistic regime. In those days, Czechs and Slovaks were united in one state, but culturally they were distinct. Slovaks were intensely Catholic, and as an independent nation today, still remain one of the more devout European countries. Czechs have long been far more secular, and though their country remains culturally conservative relative to Western European nations, it is second only to France as the most atheistic nation in Europe.

The Family and the Totalitarian State

"The underground Catholic church was the main source of resistance here," a Slovak source told me. "But over there"—that is, the Czech half of the former communist state—"the Christian resistance was the Benda family."

That's not literally true. There were other Catholic and Protestant Czech dissidents, even within the Charter 77 movement, which the Bendas helped lead. But the Slovak's rhetorical exaggeration nevertheless says something about the esteem in which this one Prague family is held in the hearts and minds of many who fought communism in their country.

Václav Benda, the father of six children, believed that the family is the bedrock of civilization, and must be nurtured and protected at all costs. He was acutely conscious of the threat communism posed to the family, and he thought deeply about the role the traditional family should take in building anti-communist Christian resistance. In the winter of 1987 to 1988, Benda wrote a short essay titled "The Family and the Totalitarian State," in which he explained his core beliefs and what must be done to help the family endure in the face of a government and a social order bent on its destruction.[1]

In the essay, Benda said that we must throw away "the regular clichés about liberation" from the traditional obligations of marriage and family. In the Christian model, marriage and family offers three gifts that are urgently needed for believers struggling within a totalitarian order.

The first is the fruitful fellowship of love

> in which we are bound together with our neighbor without pardon by virtue simply of our closeness; not on the basis of merit, rights and entitlements, but by virtue of mutual need and its affectionate reciprocation—incidentally, although completely unmotivated by notions of equality and permanent conflict between the sexes.[2]

The second gift is freedom

> given to us so absolutely that even as finite and, in the course of the conditions of the world, seemingly rooted beings, we are able to make permanent, eternal decisions; every marriage promise that is kept, every fidelity in defiance of adversity, is a radical defiance of our finitude, something that elevates us—and with us all created corporeally—higher than the angels.[3]

The third gift is the dignity of the individual within family fellowship.

In practically all other social roles we are replaceable and can be relieved of them, whether rightly or wrongly. However, such a cold calculation of justice does not reign between husband and wife, between children and parents, but rather the law of love. Even where love fails completely . . . and with all that accompanies that failure, the appeal of shared responsibility for mutual salvation remains, preventing us from giving up on unworthy sons, cheating wives, and doddering fathers.[4]

Benda was no utopian about the family. He acknowledged that families are all too human and filled with failure and weakness. In the past, though, the family could depend on the outside world to support its mission—and in turn, strong families produced citizens capable of building strong civil societies. Under communism, however, the family came under direct and sustained assault by the government, which saw its sovereignty as a threat to state control of all individuals. Writes Benda: "A left-wing intellectual terror achieved what it wanted: marriage and the family became extremely problematic institutions."

Traditional families, Christian and otherwise, living in the postcommunist liberal capitalism of today know all too well that the left-wing assault on traditional marriage and family commenced in the West with the sexual revolution in the 1960s.

It continues today in the form of direct attacks by the woke Left, including law professors advocating legal structures that dismantle the traditional family as an oppressive institution. More ominously, it comes from policies, laws, and court decisions that diminish or sever parental rights in cases involving transgender minors.

But it doesn't only come from the Left. With the advance of

consumerism and individualism, we have built a social ecosystem in which the function of the family has been reduced to producing autonomous consumers, with no sense of connection or obligation to anything greater than fulfilling their own desires. Conservative parents are often quick to spot threats to their family's values from progressive ideologues, but they can be uncritically accepting of the free market's logic and values, to say nothing of mindlessly surrendering their children's minds to smartphones and the internet.

That's why Václav Benda's advice to families living under attack from totalitarian communism remains piercingly relevant to families today.

The modern family will not hold together if the father and mother consider divorce an easy solution to marriage's difficulties. Nor, said Benda, can a family endure if the children make a mockery of the idea of marriage. When a family's members accept a culture of "sexual extravagance, promiscuity, relationships easily entered into and broken off, [and] disrespect for life" (that is, abortion), then they cannot expect the family to be what it is supposed to be and to do what it must do.

Sometimes these things appear in family life because of individual moral failures, and sometimes they manifest because of external conditions, both economic and social. There are some things we can control, Benda says, and some things that we cannot. We have to keep our ideals grounded in realism and in an awareness of our limits. Families must allow for "neither patriarchal tyranny nor crazy feminist excesses," and also reject "the worshiping of children" and catering to their every desire.

And though a strong leader within his own family, Benda grasped that the Christian father must above all be a servant of Christ.

The family cannot survive as a community if the head and center is one of its own members. The Christian statement is simple; it has to be Christ who is the true center, and in His service the individual members of this community share in the work of their salvation. One hopes that the well-grounded family can exist even without this distinctively religious affiliation; however, the focus of service to something "beyond," whether we call it love, truth or anything else, seems essential.[5]

Benda said that the family house must be a real home, "that is, a place which is livable and set apart, sheltered from the outer world; a place which is a starting-out point for adventures and experiences with the assurance of a safe return"—in other words, a haven in a heartless world. The loving, secure Christian home is a place that forms children who are capable of loving and serving others within the family, the church, the neighborhood, and indeed the nation. The family does not exist for itself alone, but first for God, and then for the sake of the broader community—a family of families.

When that nation and its people are held captive by a totalitarian order, then Christians and their families must push as hard against the totalitarian world as it pushes against them. That's what the Benda patriarch taught, and that's how he and his family lived.

Benda survived to see the fall of communism in 1989, and his friend and close collaborator Václav Havel became the first president of a free Czechoslovakia (and presided over the peaceful separation of the Czech and Slovak nations). Benda stayed active in Czech politics until his death in 1999. His widow, Kamila, still lives in the book-lined Prague apartment where, under communism, she and her husband hosted seminars for dissidents.

A Benda Guide to Child-Raising

I first visited Kamila at the family's Prague apartment in the spring of 2018 to pay my respects to the memory of her late husband. His ideas informed my own Benedict Option project, which aims at building strong Christian communities in the West's post-Christian culture. She invited some of her adult children, and grandchildren, for the evening. We gathered in the parlor of her flat, with bookshelves bearing thousands of volumes reaching from floor to ceiling, framed family photos scattered around, and a huge plaster crucifix hanging on the wall.

That Sunday evening, I learned that Václav and Kamila had not only raised children who kept the Christian faith under communist persecution, but also that their brood stayed faithful after communism, even though the overwhelming majority of their fellow Czechs had turned their backs on God. What's more, all the Benda grandchildren are also practicing Catholics.

The Benda family apartment is near the former headquarters of the StB (Státní bezpečnost), the communist-era secret police. Under the dictatorship, people who had been summoned for interrogation would sometimes stop at the Bendas' for advice about how to endure what was about to come without breaking, and to receive encouragement. Those same people would stop at the apartment for comfort after their ordeal. What the Benda family gave to the resisters was more than mere Christian hospitality.

On that first visit, and in two subsequent meetings with Benda family members, I was eager to learn how Václav and Kamila led their family to build up the inner strength of their children, not only as faithful Catholics but also as young people who understood the meaning of their parents' mission—and the sacrifices it would necessarily entail. Here is the advice they give.

MODEL MORAL COURAGE

"Our parents were heroes for us," says Patrik. "My father was the sheriff from the *High Noon* movie."

Václav often taught his children how to read the world around them, and how to understand people and events in terms of right and wrong. He did not allow them to drift into ignorance or indifference. The battle into which all of them had been thrown by history was too important.

For example, Václav explained to his kids that there are some things more dangerous than the loss of political liberties.

"Our father told us that there is a difference between a dictatorship and totalitarianism," says Marek. "Dictatorship can make life hard for you, but they don't want to devour your soul. Totalitarian regimes are seeking your souls. We have to know that so we can protect what is most important as Christians."

Watching how his brothers behaved in their adolescent years revealed to Patrik how much moral authority his father had within the family. Rebellion against authority is normal for kids that age, but the children of dissidents didn't have that luxury.

"All the arguments within the family had to be put aside so we could stand against the outside threat from communism," Patrik says. "When my father told my brother Martin that he couldn't drink alcohol publicly until he turned eighteen, he explained that this rule is a way of protecting the whole family against the regime. 'You can't do that,' he said to Martin, 'because it could endanger all of us.'"

Rather than regarding this as a heavy yoke, the Benda kids saw it as an opportunity to serve something greater than themselves.

"Watching *High Noon* really formed our way of fighting against evil," Marek Benda says. "Everyone is asking the sheriff to leave so that the town will have no problems from the bad guys. But the sheriff comes back nevertheless, because his virtue and honor can't allow him to leave. He is looking for assistance, but no one wants to do that. But his wife helps him in the end. In some way, this was our family's story. This is what our father and mother did."

You shouldn't think that their father was a natural hero, cautions Martin Benda. One evening, when Kamila was late coming home, Václav kept a nervous vigil by the window, staring at the street below, afraid that his wife had been arrested by the secret police.

"That was the moment when I started to admire my father even more," says Martin. "That's when I saw that he was human. He was scared, but he did not want his fear to master him."

FILL THEIR MORAL IMAGINATIONS WITH THE GOOD

Screening *High Noon* and movies like it for their children wasn't the only way Václav and Kamila Benda prepared them for Christian resistance. Despite the demands of her job teaching at the university,

Kamila made time to read aloud to her children for two to three hours daily.

"Every day?" I ask, stunned.

"Every day," she affirms.

She read them fairy tales, myths, adventure stories, and even some horror classics. More than any other novel, though, J. R. R. Tolkien's *The Lord of the Rings* was a cornerstone of her family's collective imagination.

Why Tolkien? I ask.

"Because we knew Mordor was real. We felt that their story"—that of the hobbits and others resisting the evil Sauron—"was our story too. Tolkien's dragons are more realistic than a lot of things we have in this world."

"Mom read *The Lord of the Rings* to us maybe six times," recalls Philip Benda. "It's about the East versus the West. The elves on one side and the goblins on the other. And when you know the book, you see that you first need to fight the evil empire, but that's not the end of the war. Afterward, you have to solve the problems at home, within the Shire."

This is how Tolkien prepared the Benda children to resist communism, and also to resist the idea that the fall of communism was the end of their quest for the Good and the True. After communism's collapse, they found ways to contribute to the moral reconstruction of their nation.

Patrik says the key is to expose children to stories that help them know the difference between truth and falsehood, and teach them how to discern this in real life.

"What my mom always encouraged in us and supported was our imagination, through the reading of books or playing with figures," he says. "She also taught us that the imagination was something that was wholly ours, that could not be stolen from us. Which was also something that differentiated us from others."

DON'T BE AFRAID TO BE WEIRD IN SOCIETY'S EYES

"In our classes at school, where we were different, we were different through our faith but also through our clothes," says Patrik. "We had more variety of our clothing, because something came from our aunt or someone who gave us our clothing. We were not hurt by being different because we considered this exceptionality was a value and not something bad."

In this way, the Benda children say their parents vaccinated them against the disease of communist ideology, which was everywhere. They brought them up to understand that they, as Christians, were not to go along to get along in their totalitarian society. Václav and Kamila knew that if they did not strongly impart that sense of difference to their children, they risked losing them to propaganda and to widespread conformity to the totalitarian system.

"Sometimes it was really hard," muses Patrik. "We were poor, and we felt the difference. It was totally impossible to buy anything fashionable, or to take part in any fad that was popular. Collectible toys that every child had, we didn't. Sometimes it was hard, but it made us stronger."

PREPARE TO MAKE GREAT SACRIFICES FOR THE GREATER GOOD

Kamila once received a letter from her husband in prison, in which he said that the government was talking about the possibility of setting him free early if he agreed to emigrate with his family to the West.

"I wrote back to tell him no, that he would be better off staying in prison to fight for what we believe is true," she tells me.

Think of it: This woman was raising six children alone, in a communist totalitarian state. But she affirmed by her own willingness to sacrifice—and to sacrifice a materially more comfortable and politically free life for her children—for the greater good.

If you fail to do this, thinking that you are making things easier for your kids, it might backfire in a big way.

"We knew people who gave in for the sake of their children," says Patrik. "They wanted their children to have a better education, so they compromised their values and entered the Communist Party. But in the end, they alienated themselves from their own children. I saw this when I was in college in 1989, during the Velvet Revolution. Some students positively hated their parents who made those compromises for them."

Today, the children and grandchildren of Dr. Benda have the letters he sent to their mother and grandmother, respectively, from prison. They are a written testimony of how the political prisoner's rock-solid faith helped him endure captivity. These letters are a catechism for his descendants, made vivid because they came from the pen not of a plaster saint, but a flesh-and-blood hero.

"In one of his letters, he tells us about how being in prison gave him new insights into the Gospels," says Patrik. "He talks about how Jesus said in his Passion, 'Not my will, but Thy will be done, Father.' My dad's letter shows how he believed that he was giving testimony by suffering persecution. This helped us all to understand the example of the Lord."

"Dad believed that even though things were bad, and he was suffering, and that he didn't see positive consequences from his actions, that there is a good God who will eventually win the battle," adds Marketa, one of the Benda daughters. "God will eventually win, even though I may not see it in my life. So my suffering is not meaningless, because I am part of a greater battle that will be victorious in the end. That is what our father showed us by his life."

"But father believed that the communists would fall, and that he would live to see it happen," says Patrik.

"That's true," says Kamila. "But he also had the conviction that to destroy the communist regime was his mission in life. He was always talking with God and asking what is the right way. He always struggled to see the right values, and to live up to them."

"This is something very important about my father," says Marketa. "He believed that he was accountable before God, not before people. It didn't matter to him when other people didn't understand why he did the things he did. He acted in the sight of God. And you know, the Bible gave him strength, because it is full of stories of the prophets and others going beyond the border of what was comprehensible or understandable to people, for the sake of obeying the Lord."

TEACH THEY ARE PART OF A WIDER MOVEMENT

The Bendas were founding members of Charter 77, the main Czechoslovak dissident community. Charter 77 was a 1977 document signed by over two hundred artists, intellectuals, and others, demanding that the communist regime respect human rights. Some of its signatories, including the playwright and future president Václav Havel, and Václav Benda, landed in prison for their advocacy.

"We pulled our children into our struggles," says Kamila. "They had the feeling that we were all members of a group and had a common goal. They were raised to know that they were fighting for a good cause, for justice."

It was not just a matter of holding the correct opinions and proper sentiments. The Benda children took risks on behalf of the resistance.

"Sometimes when we wanted to send something confidential, we would send one of the kids, because it was less likely that he would be captured," recalls Kamila. "They also learned to swallow small pieces of paper with messages written on them if there was a danger of arrest."

Being active in a wider movement for liberty, democracy, and human rights helped shape the Benda children in other ways. Though Václav and Kamila Benda held their Catholic beliefs uncompromisingly within the family, they showed their children by example the importance of working with good and decent people outside the moral and theological community of the church.

Patrik reminds me that his family were the only Christians involved in the movement in Prague. All other senior Charter 77 members were secular. Though most were strongly anti-communist in one way or another, one, Petr Uhl, was a self-described "revolutionary Marxist," but one who believed that a Marxist state without human rights is not worth fighting for.

"In Charter 77, you had people of totally different worldviews and ideas joined together," says Patrik. "You had, for example, democratic socialists on the one side and fervent Catholics on the other side. It was totally normal for me that as a small child, I was being raised in a community of people with very different opinions. So it shattered the bubble around me."

The lesson of valuing diversity within a broader unity of shared goals is something that Christians today need to embrace.

"When we look at what's happening in America today, we see that you are building walls and creating gaps between people," he says. "For us, we are always willing to speak, to talk with the other side to avoid building walls between people. You know, it is much easier to indoctrinate someone who is enclosed within a set of walls."

PRACTICE HOSPITALITY AND SERVE OTHERS

Kamila says that obeying Christ's command to love one's neighbor means never failing to stand up for every persecuted person, not just churchgoers. She brought up the people who would come by their apartment on their way to interrogation. Kamila was a den-mother figure who would share with them strategies for enduring police questioning, which could be quite harsh, without surrendering information.

Up to twenty people would show up every day at the Benda flat, seeking advice, comfort, and community. And after police released the suspects, they would often return to the Benda home. Whether or not they had come through without breaking, or had given up information under duress, Kamila offered them a cup of tea and a glass of wine and encouragement.

"Mom would tell them, 'That's okay, next time, you will do better,'" says Patrik. The dissident circle was too small and fragile to turn on one another, despite their failures, frustrations, and disappointments.

Kamila and I talk again about the communist-era teaching seminars the Bendas held in their apartment. It's a practice her adult children have taken up. These days, Marketa hosts similar gatherings in the family apartment.

"She calls her salon Evenings with Cheese," said Marketa's niece, Klara, "because of her nickname. They call her 'Mouse.' She invites people she knows from the university, or through her work, and they will all talk about what they are doing."

Patrik, who is also a host, says they screen a film once a month and invite groups of people to come watch it and talk about it. Sure, he says, you can watch anything you like in your own home, but there's something unique about sharing the experience with others, and talking about it.

"I think one of the important things about this is that people actually like to meet and want to meet, but when you don't have a subject to form the meeting around, it usually goes to waste," says Klara, Patrik's teenage daughter. "When you have the movie, then you can start from the movie. We end up having a conversation about high school exams and how much we hate them. That's great, but the point is, you have to start from somewhere real."

I mention Václav Benda's well-known idea that in a society of atomized individuals, as communist Czechoslovakia was, it was important for ordinary people to come together and to be reminded of one another's existence. In a time when people have forgotten how to be neighbors, simply sharing a meal or a movie together is a political act. This, I say, is a way to fight back against the loneliness and isolation that allows totalitarianism to rule.

That's true, says Patrik, but it is also the case that talking about movies is a way for older members of the community to contribute to the passing on of cultural memory to the young.

"I had the experience with some people who are twenty years younger than me consider a movie great and interesting, but they don't know that it's a remake of something older," he says. "Also, we don't just screen new movies but also older ones. Jumping between eras helps the young people to understand the cultural context in which the films are made. The fact that the younger ones can learn from the knowledge and experience of the older ones is really meaningful."

For the Benda family of Prague, their purpose is first to serve God and then to serve others. They did this under communism, and they are doing it under post-Christian liberalism. It's a family tradition.

The Social Importance of Family

The Bendas were not the only family resisting communism. In many conversations throughout the former Soviet Bloc, I heard stories of how the Christian family was naturally the bedrock of forming faithful resistance to communism.

In Russia, you expect to find Orthodox Christians, but Baptists are much rarer. They were unknown in this country until the latter half of the nineteenth century, and even today are only about seventy-six thousand in a vast nation of 145 million souls. A gentle, white-haired pastor named Yuri Sipko was once the leader of his country's Baptists.

It was a difficult job, even after the collapse of Soviet power. Baptists are marginalized and at times persecuted in Russia, even by other believers. Under communism, though, they not only had to contend with ostracism from fellow Christians, but like all other religious believers, were also severely attacked by the Soviet state. Communist propaganda depicted Baptists as members of a dangerous, primitive cult. Sipko, born in 1952 into a family of twelve children, says his father and mother planted the seeds of courage in his heart.

"My father was the pastor of our congregation. All sorts of pressure was put on him," Sipko recalls. "When I was a child, all I knew was that I wanted to be like my father. I saw that he was able to stand alone, with dignity and courage, against all his enemies."

When Yuri was still a boy, the Soviets sent his father to prison for five years for preaching. His mother, along with several other women in the congregation, was left alone to raise the children. These mothers read the Bible to the kids, prayed with them, wept with them, and taught their little ones what to live for.

One day, Yuri's teacher called his mother to the school for a conference. The teacher was angry because the child refused to accept the state-mandated lessons in atheism and materialism. Yuri's teacher demanded to know what kind of cult Mrs. Sipko belonged to and why they taught children such nonsense. The boy watched his mother, whose husband was in prison for his faith, to see how she would react to this dressing-down by an authority figure.

146

"She got out her Bible and began to read," he remembers, smiling. "It makes me so happy to think about it. The teacher called me to her and said, 'This is *our* boy. He's learning *our* lessons.' But under the protection of my mother, I found the courage to say, 'No, I believe in God.' It was a fiasco for the teacher."

In a vastly more consequential way, Polish authorities plunged headlong into a similar fiasco when they crushed Father Jerzy Popiełuszko, who was chaplain to Poland's trade union, Solidarity. Despite numerous threats to his life, the Warsaw priest spoke out against the criminal regime. In 1984, the secret police murdered him and dumped his body in a river.

Father Jerzy was a mediocre seminary student and an undistinguished priest—until the rise of Solidarity in opposition to communist brutality called him to his destiny.

Paweł Kęska, who directs the Popiełuszko museum in the martyred priest's Warsaw parish, told me a story about nearly one million mourners who came to Father Jerzy's funeral. And then he told me a story about the modest childhood of the priest who would become a national hero, and who is on his way to official sainthood in the Catholic Church.

Kęska said that the impoverished rural village where Father Jerzy was born is nothing special. Kęska had recently returned from a pilgrimage there with a student group.

"The village is very ordinary—there's nothing spiritual there," Kęska told me. "In the home where Father Jerzy lived, there's one room that has been set apart as a kind of museum, but all the items there are under a thick veil of dust. By the wall is a small table, covered with a kind of plastic sheet. There is a small piece of paper with handwriting on it, written by Father Jerzy's brother. It said, 'Every day near the table we were praying with our mother.' There is a photo of that mother as an old, tired woman. On the other side of that piece of paper is a reliquary with Father Jerzy's relics."

Father Jerzy's ended his short life as a national hero of Christian resistance to communism, beloved by millions for his fidelity to God and his willingness to risk his own life to speak out against injustice to others. But it began in a little house in a dull, poor village in the middle of nowhere, in the bosom of a family that prayed together.

"And that's the answer," Kęska concluded. "The whole strength of that man, and what we need today for our identity."

"It's no accident that every dictatorship always tries to break down the family, because it's in the family that you get the strength to be able to fight," says Mária Komáromi, a Catholic teacher in Budapest. "You have the feeling that they have your back, so you can go out into the world and face anything. It's just as true today as it was under communism."

Over and over in my travels in the East, survivors of communism emphasized to me how much more difficult it is to identify the threats against faith and family today than it was under communism. But it is no less necessary to do so—and to do so with discipline, not relying only on sentimentality, but with a hard charity, the only kind that endures.

Tertullian, an early Church Father who wrote under Roman persecution, famously said that the willingness of martyrs to suffer—even unto death—is what plants love of God into the hearts of men. That may be true, but as the stories of the families Benda, Sipko, Popiełuszko, and so many other conquerors of communism show, the love of mothers and fathers is the seed of the church.

See, Judge, Act

In the coming soft totalitarianism, Christians will have to regard family life in a much more focused, serious way. The traditional Christian family is not merely a good idea—it is also a survival strategy for the faith in a time of persecution. Christians should stop taking family life for granted, instead approaching it in a more thoughtful, disciplined way. We cannot simply live as all other families live, except that we go to church on Sunday. Holding the correct theological beliefs and having the right intentions will not be enough. Christian parents must be intentionally countercultural in their approach to family dynamics. The days of living like everybody else and hoping our children turn out for the best are over.

The Benda family model requires parents to exercise discernment. For example, the Bendas didn't opt out of popular culture but rather chose intelligently which parts of it they wanted their children to absorb. To visit the Benda family home is not to step into a Spartan barracks but rather into a place filled with books and art and life. The Benda family judged that they could be open to the good things in the world around them because of the disciplined moral, intellectual, and spiritual lives they lived within the family.

And they acted with openness to the world. Václav Benda taught that the family does not exist for its own purpose but for the service of something beyond itself. When you pay a call on Kamila, you sit on chairs and sofas that are well worn from years of hosting guests invited to share in the joy of her clan's Christian lives. True, they had to judge carefully who to let into their home and what to say around them, but there was no doubt in the minds of Václav and Kamila Benda that their role as Christians was not to draw the shutters and hide, as so many Czech Christians did, but to be of active service to the church and the world. For those who survive Václav—Kamila, her children, and grandchildren—it still is.

As we will learn in an upcoming chapter, small-group fellowship was critical to building effective Christian resistance to totalitarianism. A truth to which the Benda family, and other families that formed the consciences of other anti-communist dissidents, testify to is this: if you want to love and serve the church, the community, and the nation, you must first learn to love and serve your family.

CHAPTER EIGHT

Religion, the Bedrock of Resistance

Not every anti-communist dissident was a Christian, and not every Christian living under communist totalitarianism resisted. But here's an interesting thing: every single Christian I interviewed for this book, in every ex-communist country, conveyed a sense of deep inner peace—a peace that they credit to their faith, which gave them ground on which to stand firm.

They had every right to be permanently angry over what had been done to them, to their families, their churches, and their countries. If they were, it didn't show. A former prisoner of conscience in Russia told me that Christians need to have "a golden dream—something to live for, a conception of hope. You can't simply be against everything bad. You have to be for something good. Otherwise, you can get really dark and crazy."

This is the core of what religion brings to anti-totalitarian resistance: a reason to die—which is to say, a reason to live with whatever suffering the regime throws at you, and not only to live, but to thrive.

This is not to say that Christianity's *only* value is in its usefulness to anti-communists. Any contrary belief held with the passionate inwardness of religious faith could serve that purpose. To give the devil his due, the tsarist-era young Bolsheviks endured their miserable Siberian exile like champions because they held their principles with religious fervor. The important lesson to draw is that a creed one holds as statement not of one's subjective feelings, but as a description of objective reality, is a priceless possession. It tells you how to discern truth from lies. And for those whose creed is Christianity, then in the face of ubiquitous hatred and cruelty, faith is evidence that the true Truth, the real Reality, is the eternal love of God.

The Spiritual Exercises of the Prisoner Krčméry

In totalitarian Czechoslovakia, Kolaković follower Silvester Krčméry (pronounced "kirch-MERRY") emerged as one of the priest's most important disciples and organizers. Years of Bible study, worship, and personal spiritual practice under the guidance of Father Kolaković prepared the young physician for a long prison term, which began with his arrest in 1951.

The basis for his resistance was the firm conviction that "there could not be anything more beautiful than to lay down my life for God." When that thought came to Krčméry in the police sedan minutes after his arrest, he burst into laughter. His captors were not amused. But refusing self-pity, and teaching himself to receive whatever the interrogators did to him as an aid to his own salvation, saved Krčméry's spiritual life.

Behind bars, and subject to all manner of torture and humiliation, Krčméry kept himself sane and hopeful through cultivating and practicing his faith in a disciplined way and by evangelizing others.

In his memoir, *This Saved Us*, Krčméry recalls that after repeated beatings, torture, and interrogations, he realized that the only way he would make it through the ordeal ahead was to rely entirely on faith, not reason. He says he decided to be "like Peter, to close my eyes and throw myself into the sea."

> In my case, it truly was to plunge into physical and spiritual uncertainty, an abyss, where only faith in God could guarantee safety. Material things which mankind regarded as certainties were fleeting and illusory, while faith, which the world considered to be ephemeral, was the most reliable and the most powerful of foundations.
>
> The more I depended on faith, the stronger I became.[1]

His personal routine included memorizing passages from a New Testament a new prisoner had smuggled into the jail. The Scripture Krčméry had already learned before the persecution started turned out to be a powerful aid behind bars.

"Memorizing texts from the New Testament proved to be an excellent preparation for critical times and imprisonment," he writes. "The most beautiful and important texts which mankind has from God contain a priceless treasure which 'moth and decay cannot destroy, and thieves break in and steal' (Matthew 6:19)."

Committing Scripture to memory formed a strong basis for prison life, the doctor found.

"Indeed, as one's spiritual life intensifies, things become clearer and the essence of God is more easily understood," he writes. "Sometimes one word, or a single sentence from Scripture, is enough to fill a person with a special light. An insight or new meaning is revealed and penetrates one's inner being and remains there for weeks or months at a time."[2]

Krčméry structured his days and weeks to pray the Catholic mass, and sometimes the Orthodox Divine Liturgy. He interceded for specific people and groups of people, including his captors. This was a way of ordering the oppressive expanse of time, especially during periods of solitary confinement. Krčméry and his fellow prisoners were astonished, repeatedly, that beatings and interrogations were easier to endure than seemingly ceaseless periods of waiting.

The prisoner did periods of deep, sustained meditation, in which he thought deeply about his own life and his own sins, and he embraced a spirit of repentance. At one point, Krčméry wondered if he was wasting his time and increasing his emotional and psychological burden by sticking to these daylong spiritual exercises.

"I attempted to live a few days entirely without a program, but it did not work," he remembers. "When I thought that I would only vegetate for the whole day, and just rest, that is when there were the most crises."

Along with other prisoners, Krčméry would sing hymns, and would pray litanies for everyday needs, including for a spirit of humility and willingness to endure all for the sake of Christ. This brotherhood was an integral part of the spirituality of Christian resistance. Father Kolaković had taught the Family the virtue of reaching across church lines to establish brotherhood with other Christians. Captivity and torture turned this into a practical reality.

"In prison, nobody recognized any confessional differences," writes Krčméry.

This same principle echoes in the testimony of the Lutheran pastor Richard Wurmbrand and other former captives of the communists. It is not a false ecumenism that claims all religions are essentially the same. It is rather a mutual recognition that within the context of persecution, embracing Jan Patočka's "solidarity of the shattered" becomes vital to spiritual survival.

Silvester Krčméry left prison in 1964. He spent the next twenty-five years continuing his work for the anti-communist resistance. Along with other veterans of the underground church, he was a principal organizer of the 1988 Candle Demonstration in Bratislava, the Slovak capital. It was the first mass protest in Czechoslovakia in almost two decades, and served as a catalyst to the 1989 Velvet Revolution that restored freedom and democracy.

The Power of the Powerless Church

Patrick Parkinson is an Evangelical Christian and dean of one of Australia's top law schools. He lived in Bratislava as a student in the early 1980s, and witnessed the spiritual power of the underground church firsthand. In a world of despair, these believers provided something rare and precious: real hope, the living out of which risked their lives and freedom.

"The church in those times offered people an alternative worldview," Professor Parkinson tells me. "My young Catholic friends in the university, in particular, demonstrated great courage and faith. Their core instruction was to read the Bible every day and to pray every day at nine p.m. for the suffering church. They risked much to meet in small Bible study and prayer groups and security was very tight, but God protected them in wonderful ways."

Nearly four decades later, Parkinson looks to the young Slovak Christians of his youth for hope in our own dark and difficult days. "There was a hunger for God when I was there, which I attributed in no small part to the enormous disillusionment with communism," he says. "Disillusionment with materialism may take another couple of generations."

When it comes, Christians who proclaimed with their words and deeds a real alternative to hedonistic materialism will be beacons guiding the lost and tempest-tossed.

Father Dmitry Dudko, who died in 2004, was a Russian Orthodox priest who, with astonishing courage, stood up to Soviet authorities for the sake of the Gospel. In the early 1970s, Father Dmitry became one of the best-known dissident Christians in the USSR. Before ordination, he spent eight years in the gulag for having written a poem critical of Stalin; a fellow seminarian turned him in. He was eventually made a priest, but remained under close KGB surveillance.

Stricken by grief over the spiritual desolation and resulting alcoholism ravaging the Soviet Union, Father Dmitry grew increasingly bold in his evangelism. He began giving bold sermons in his Moscow parish, homilies that brought Christian teaching to bear on real-life problems. Word spread that there was a priest unafraid to speak to the real suffering of the people. Crowds began coming to hear the prophetic cleric. When the institutional church, which was under KGB control, ordered Father Dmitry to stop using homilies to stir up congregations, he continued his talks at home.

In his 2014 book about Father Dmitry, *The Last Man in Russia*, journalist Oliver Bullough quotes an atheist saying that after hearing the priest preach, "the immorality of Soviet society, its inhumanity and corruption, its lack of a moral code or credible ideals, means that Christ's teaching comes through to those who it reaches as a shining contrast. It stresses the value of the individual, of humanness, forgiveness, gentleness, love."[3]

Another witness said that "when Father Dmitry answered our questions publicly, it was like a mouthful of water." The priest stressed to his audiences that they needed to cultivate hope that tomorrow can be better, and that they must embrace the suffering and love them into healing. Bullough says that in 1973, when Father Dmitry's talks became known all over Moscow, the priest drew atheists, intellectuals, Christians of all denominations, and even Jews and Marxists.

Why did they come? Because they lived in a total system that insisted that it had all the answers to life's questions. But the people, they were completely miserable, and lost, and in pain. They knew it was all a lie, because they were living within that dark lie. They were drawn to people who looked like they were living in the light of truth.

Alexander Ogorodnikov was a celebrated Soviet youth leader who, having become disillusioned by communism, devoted his passion to serving the church by creating independent discussion groups. In our Moscow meeting, he tells me that at one of his seminars there appeared an elderly writer who sat listening to the young Christians—every single one of them had been atheists from good Soviet families—talking about the faith. The visitor said not a word.

"Finally he stood up and said that he was the son of a high official of the tsar. He said, 'Brothers, you have no idea what you are doing. If just ten of you had been in Saint Petersburg in 1917, the Revolution would not have happened,'" recalls Ogorodnikov.

"That man had already been through the gulag," he continues. "He felt welcome with us. We had a really, really brotherly atmosphere in the seminars. Those seminars were like a bonfire where people could come and warm up their frozen Orthodox hearts. This was the blood that flowed in our veins. This was our confession of faith."

Viktor Popkov was one of the disillusioned young Soviets who had found his way into the tiny Christian movement of the time. I sit down with Popkov, an Orthodox Christian, in a kitchen in central Moscow. In the early 1970s, Popkov had no interest in faith. "I was just living in a swamp, trying to find just a little piece of dry land on which to stand," he says.

Nothing was real about life under communism. The state's control was total. What led Popkov to seek fellowship with Christians was reading *The Stranger*, the celebrated 1942 novel by Albert Camus, the French existentialist. Though Camus was an atheist, the novel compelled the young Russian living in an atheist state to look for Christ.

"The question stood before me: What is the point of living?" he tells me. "If Christ is real, what is that supposed to mean for me? That was my point of departure from Soviet life—and I know a lot of people who found similar points of departure."

Slowly, Popkov felt himself drawn to church. The local Orthodox priest didn't want to talk to him. If the government found out that he had been speaking to a potential convert, the priest could have been sacked. Popkov heard through the Moscow grapevine about groups of people coming together to talk about Christianity. Unfortunately, if he'd heard about it, the KGB usually had as well.

If you came to the meetings anyway, the KGB would pressure your parents and teachers to dissuade you from the faith, Popkov remembers. It was hard to deal with, "but at the same time, you gain experience of a different life. In this experience of faith and this encounter with Christ, you receive a new feeling, and you know that you would not go back to how you used to be for anything. You are willing to endure anything they throw at you."

"You can't really prepare for it," he went on. "To have a living connection to Christ, it's like falling in love. You suddenly feel something you haven't felt before, and you're ready to do something you've never done before."

For Viktor Popkov, that meant enduring years of harassment from the secret police, culminating in a 1980 prison sentence.

"Maybe this will sound strong," he says, "but the principles and the things that you confess, you need to be ready to die for them—and only then will you have the strength to resist. I don't see any other way."

This truth is what the Romanian Orthodox priest George Calciu proclaimed to the youth in Bucharest in one of his 1978 Lenten homilies—a sermon series that earned him a second stint in prison:

> Go, young man, and tell this news to all. Let the light of your angelic face shine in the light of the Resurrection—for today the angel in you . . . has overcome the world in you. Tell those who until now have oppressed your divine soul: "I believe in the Resurrection," and you will see them

coil in fear, for your faith has overcome them. They will fret and shout to you in despair: "This earth is your paradise and your instincts are your heaven."

Do not stop on your path, but go on, shining and pure, giving the light of that Resurrection on the first of Sabbaths to all. You, my friend, are the unique bearer of your deification in Jesus Christ, and with yourself you raise up the entire Romanian people to the height of its own resurrection. From death to life and from earth to heaven![4]

Shortly after giving that sermon, the Romanian dictatorship slapped Father George with a ten-year prison sentence. He served five, was given early release, and then he was expelled to the United States by the regime.

The Miracle of the Cigarettes

If you believe that God exists, then you must also believe that miracles are possible. Christians live by faith, but sometimes, God sends a message to remind us that he exists and has not abandoned us. Drinking tea in the lobby of a Moscow hotel, Alexander Ogorodnikov tells a story about an extremely improbable thing that happened to him upon entering a Soviet prison—something that signaled to him that God led him to that vault of human misery for a higher purpose.

"When they put me in the cell with the other inmates, I said,

'Peace be with you!'" Ogorodnikov remembers. "One of the prisoners asked if I was a Christian. I said yes. He told me to prove it. Another inmate said, 'We are the scum of the earth. We don't even have cigarettes. If your God will give us cigarettes, we'll all believe in him.'"

Ogorodnikov told his fellow prisoners that the body is the temple of the Holy Spirit, and smoking fouls it. But, he continued, God loves you so much that I believe he would even give you cigarettes as a sign of his mercy. Ogorodnikov asked them all to stand and pray together for this. Everybody laughed, but they stood respectfully as he led them in prayer.

"That cell was very crowded, but it became very quiet," he recalls. "We prayed for fifteen minutes, then I told them the prayer was over and they could sit down. At just that moment, the guards opened the cell door and threw a bunch of cigarettes into the cell."

"That really happened?!" I ask, astonished.

"That really happened," he answers. "It was incredible. There was the sign I had prayed for. The prisoners shouted, 'God exists! He exists!' And that is when I knew that God was speaking to me too. He was telling me that he had a mission for me here in this prison."

Alexander Ogorodnikov thus began his life hidden behind the walls of the Soviet prison system. But he was not hidden from God. And because of that, as the Christian dissident would learn, God manifested through his fidelity to those damned to die before a firing squad who were desperate for a sign of hope. Ogorodnikov's connection to God would be, to these wretched men, their only lifeline.

See, Judge, Act

A time of painful testing, even persecution, is coming. Lukewarm or shallow Christians will not come through with their faith intact. Christians today must dig deep into the Bible and church tradition and teach themselves how and why today's post-Christian world, with its self-centeredness, its quest for happiness and rejection of sacred order and transcendent values, is a rival religion to authentic Christianity. We should also see how many of the world's values have been absorbed into Christian life and practice.

Then we must judge how the ways of the world, and its demands, conflict with what Christ requires of his disciples. Are we admirers, or followers? How will we know?

We will know when we act—or fail to act—as Christians when to be faithful costs us something. It may be a small thing at first— a place on a sports team because we won't play on Sunday mornings, or the respect of our peers when we will not march in a parade for a political cause. But the demands made on us will grow greater, and the consequences for failing to submit to the world's demands will grow more severe. Father Kolaković told his Family this—and in a way, he's telling us the same thing today.

We serve a God who created all things for a purpose. He has shown us in the Bible, especially the Gospels, who we are and how we are to live to be in harmony with the sacred order he created. He does not want admirers; he wants followers. As Jesus Christ, the Second Person of the Holy Trinity, God suffered with humanity to redeem humanity. He calls us to share in his Passion, for our sake and the sake of the world. He promises us nothing but the cross. Not happiness but the joy of blessedness. Not material wealth but richness of spirit. Not sexual freedom as erotic abandon but sexual freedom within loving, mutually sacrificial commitment. Not power but love; not self-sovereignty but obedience.

This is the uncompromising rival religion that the post-Christian world will not long tolerate. If you are not rock solid in your commitment to traditional Christianity, then the world will break you. But if you are, then this is the solid rock upon which that world will be broken. And if those solid rocks are joined together, they form a wall of solidarity that is very hard for the enemy to breach.

CHAPTER NINE

Standing in Solidarity

Now for the first time you were about to see people
who were not your enemies. Now for the first time
you were about to see others who were alive, who
were traveling your road, and whom you could
join to yourself with the joyous word "we."

**ALEKSANDR SOLZHENITSYN,
ON ARRIVING IN ONE'S FIRST PRISON CELL,
IN *THE GULAG ARCHIPELAGO*[1]**

The house is like every other house on this unremarkable street
in suburban Bratislava. We walk through the back garden,
past the lawn furniture and the children's toys. Ján Šimulčik,
a Slovak historian of the underground church, knocks on the door.
He has arranged with the mother who lives here with her husband
and kids to show his American visitor what makes this house different from all others in the neighborhood.

In the 1980s, this house was a headquarters for printing and distributing Christian samizdat—underground literature forbidden by the communist regime. Šimulčik, now in his fifties, was part of the movement as a college student. A Catholic priest posing as a worker lived in secret in the house back then. Šimulčik and a handful of other Catholic students would come there at planned intervals to sort and package samizdat documents for distribution.

Šimulčik leads me down a crumbling concrete staircase into a basement. It is plain, damp, and a bit chilly, like every other basement in the world. What is his point? I wonder.

Then the scholar removes a floor panel that had entirely escaped my notice. There is a hole in the basement floor big enough for a man to climb through, and iron rungs embedded in the concrete wall. Šimulčik turns around backward and descends into the hole, signaling for me to follow.

At the bottom there is a short tunnel. Crouching to make my way through the cramped space, I follow Šimulčik up the iron rungs in the exit shaft. We emerge into a tiny room, not much bigger than a closet. There is a table against the wall, upon which sits an offset printing machine of 1980 vintage.

In this secret room, underneath the house and behind a secret basement wall, accessible only by hidden tunnel, dissident Christians printed Gospels, prayer books, and catechism lessons for clandestine distribution throughout communist Slovakia. The printer was a gift to the Catholics from Evangelical Christians in the Netherlands, who smuggled it into the country in pieces and sent a second team to reassemble it in the underground room.

After communism fell in 1989, the operation ended and the undercover priest moved out of the house. But subsequent owners have maintained the secret room as a reminder of what it took to save the faith under the totalitarian yoke.

"There was a man at my university who worked as an elevator repairman," Šimulčik tells me as we stand in the room, our heads almost touching the ceiling. "His hands were often stained. I thought it was from the grease and the grime of repairing elevators, but it was actually from the ink he used to print samizdat. His job was the perfect cover."

As a student, Šimulčik knew that the elevator repairman had something to do with the Christian underground, but he wasn't sure what. That was by design. The underground only shared information like that on a need-to-know basis, so those arrested by the secret police couldn't compromise the operations if they broke under interrogation. What Šimulčik did not learn until communism fell was that for all those years he was upstairs in that house compiling samizdat, that elevator repairman was down below, spending hours in the tomblike room, printing the words of life at great risk to his own liberty.

In fact, everyone involved with the Christian samizdat project would have been sent to prison had the secret police ever discovered the network. As Šimulčik breaks down for me the complex moving parts of the operation, he emphasizes the extraordinary risks the underground Christians took for the sake of publishing these documents. Why did you get involved? I ask. You could have lost everything.

"When you ask that question, you are really asking about where we find the meaning of the underground church," Šimulčik replies. "It was in small community. Only in small communities could people feel free."

He goes on:

When you were with your friends in these communities, you had freedom. You knew that when you went outside, there was totalitarianism. It controlled everything and oppressed you. People like me who wanted knowledge and freedom, and wanted to know more about our faith, depended on these small communities. They were well organized, and we had strong leaders. This was the only place to find that. First, I did it because I wanted to experience personal freedom, but this was connected to Christ. After we tasted freedom in these communities, we gradually came to want to fight for freedom for everyone.

Šimulčik tells me that he and his cell of several other young Catholic men were all afraid. You would have been crazy not to have fear.

"The question is, which is going to win: fear, or courage?" he says. "In the beginning, it was mostly a matter of fear. But once you started experiencing freedom—and you felt it, you *felt* freedom through the things you did—your courage grew. We experienced all this together. We helped one another to gradually build up the courage to do bigger things, like join the Candle Demonstration."

"With this courage also developed our sense of duty, and our need to be of service to other people," the historian continues. "We could see the products of our work. We could hold these samizdat books in our hands, and we could see that people really read them and learned from them. We saw what we did as service to God and service to people. But it took years for us to see the fruit of our labor and to see our communities grow."

Small Communities Can Rescue the Lone Individual

František Mikloško, now in his seventies, was a central leader of the second wave of the Slovak underground church. When we meet for lunch in a Bratislava restaurant, he is quick to offer advice to the current generation of Christians, who, in his view, are facing a very different kind of challenge than he did at their age.

"When I talk to young people today, I tell them that they have it harder than we did in one way: it is harder to tell who is the enemy. I tell them that what is crucial is to stay true to yourself, true to your conscience, and also to be in community with other like-minded people who share the faith. We were saved by small communities."

Mikloško, in his youth a close aide to the underground Catholic bishop Ján Chryzostom Korec, credits the clandestine bishop—made a cardinal by Pope John Paul II after communism's fall—with emphasizing the importance of small communities.

"He told us that they"—the communists—"could take everything from us. They could take samizdat from us. They can take our opportunity to speak out publicly from us. But we can't let them take away our small communities."

Mikloško started university in Bratislava in 1966, and met the recently released prisoners Krčméry and Jukl. He was in the first small community the two Kolaković disciples founded at the university. Christians like Krčméry and Jukl brought not only their expertise in Christian resistance to a new generation but also the testimony of their character. They were like electromagnets with a powerful draw to young idealists.

"It's like in the Bible, the parable of ten righteous people," says

Mikloško. "True, in Slovakia, there were many more than ten righteous people. But ten would have been enough. You can build a whole country on ten righteous people who are like pillars, like monuments."

These early converts spread the word about the community to other towns in Slovakia, just as the Kolaković generation had done. Soon there were hundreds of young believers, sustained by prayer meetings, samizdat, and one another's fellowship.

"Finally, in 1988, the secret police called me in and said, 'Mr. Mikloško, this is it. If you all don't stop what you're doing, you will force us to act,'" he says. "But by then, there were so many people, and the network was so large, that they couldn't stop it.

"If they had come at us in the seventies, they might have succeeded. But we always remembered that the goal was to turn our small numbers into a number so big they can't stop us," Mikloško says. "Thank God we had leaders who taught us patience."

"Most of us had fear, but there were people among us who really did act absolutely fearlessly. I'm thinking about Silvo Krčméry, Vlado Jukl, Bishop Korec, but there were hundreds, even thousands of others," says historian Ján Šimulčik. "Young people like me saw their example and were able to grow in courage by their example. The lesson here is that when you *see* someone acting courageously, you will act courageously as well."

In many traditional liturgical churches, on the night of the Easter celebration, the congregation stands in total darkness, holding unlit candles. The priest takes the flame from the paschal candle, lights a few tapers held by the faithful, who turn to those around them and spread the flame. Within minutes, the lights from scores, even hundreds, perhaps, and in cathedrals, even thousands, of candles illuminate what was once a sepulchral room. This is the light that precedes the proclamation of Resurrection.

And so: In 1988, the underground church leaders, the spiritual grandchildren of Father Kolaković, organized the Candlelight Demonstration in Bratislava—the largest protest event in Czecho-slovakia since the 1960s. The police used water cannons to disperse thousands of Christians gathered peacefully on the city's main square to pray for religious and civil liberties. But it was too late for the communists: the momentum was with the people. Within two years, communism was over.

"I had the fastest rise of any modern European politician," jokes Slovak lawyer Ján Čarnogurský, a former political prisoner and a leader of the Candle Demonstration. "I was released from prison, and two weeks later, I was sitting at the table with Václav Havel negotiating with the communists about the handover of power."

Small Groups Can Be a Pastoral Lifeline

Father Kolaković's instinct to build up the Catholic laity as a source of resistance proved to be a stroke of genius.

"The official, approved Catholic Church was limited to just the churches," says Ján Čarnogurský, who defended dissidents in court. "If the priests were discovered coming to someone's apartment and praying with them, for example, they would be sentenced to prison. It was against the criminal code. It took maybe twenty years before the Catholic Church figured out how to keep the faith alive under these conditions, but it was the underground church that did it."

In Soviet Russia, Evangelicals learned and practiced this survival skill decades earlier. The Baptist pastor Yuri Sipko, now sixty-eight, recalls the world that he was born into—a world that his parents and their friends had been living in for some time under Stalin's merciless persecution of the churches.

"The strongest strike was against the preachers and the pastors, first of all. They took the preachers and pastors to prison. Other men stood up and filled their shoes," Sipko tells me. "Then they took their houses of prayer. Then at that point began the practice of small groups—people who lived close to one another would gather in small groups. There was no formal structure of pastors or deacons. There were just brothers and sisters who read the Bible together, prayed together, and sang."

"When they jailed my father, my mother was left alone," he continues. "Several other sisters were left without husbands. We all got together. We found the Bible they had hidden. The women were reading the Bible to all of us. They were telling how people should live, what we had to hope for. They prayed together, and cried."

These small groups continued the life of the Baptist church for decades, until Gorbachev released the last Evangelical prisoners of conscience.

"Sixty years of terror, they were unable to get rid of the faith," the pastor muses. "It was saved specifically in small groups. There was no literature, no organizations for teaching, and even movement was forbidden. Believers rewrote biblical texts by hand. Even the songs that we sang. I even remember writing these notebooks for myself. But they preserved the true faith."

Over steaming cups of black tea, the pastor reflects with palpable emotion.

"Many of us didn't even have Bibles. Just to be able to find yourself in a situation where there was a group, and one person was reading the Bible to others, this was the greatest motivation," Sipko says. "This was our little niche of freedom. Whether you were at work in the factory, on the street, or anywhere else, everything was godless."

Today, it is easy to obtain a Bible in Russia, easy to meet for worship services, and easy to find religious teaching on the internet. Yet something among contemporary Christians has been lost, the old pastor says—something that was held dear by those small groups.

Sipko goes on:

> Christianity has become a secondary foundation in people's lives, not the main foundation. Now it's all about career, material success, and one's standing in society. In these small groups, when people were meeting back then, the center was Christ, and his word that was being read, and being interpreted as applicable to your own life. What am I supposed to do as a Christian? What am I doing as a Christian? I, together with my brothers, was checking my own Christianity.

Small groups not only provided accountability, he says, but also gave believers a tangible connection to the larger Body of Christ. "This was so wonderful. This was true Christianity."

It was startling to hear Sipko say that in Russia today, there are Evangelicals who have returned to the patterns of life their ancestors lived under communism—even though there is far more freedom (of religion, and everything else) since the Soviet Union's demise in 1991. "They have a very clear understanding that their faith in Christ means they are going to have to reject this secular world," he says. "Even under free conditions today, we are having to live in the underground."

Though it's unlikely that American Christians will be threatened for going to church, it is not only possible, but quite likely, that institutional churches and their ministers will continue to be inadequate to the challenge of forming their congregations for effective resistance. This is where intense, committed small groups styled after those of the Soviet era could be indispensable.

Small groups are not new. In the United States, Evangelical and charismatic congregations have long practiced meeting in small groups outside of formal worship for prayer and discipleship. What the experience of the church under communism, and a discerning read of the signs of the times today, tells us is that all Christians of every church should start forming these cells—not simply to deepen its members' spiritual lives, but to train them in active resistance.

Solidarity Is Not Exclusively Christian

As important as it is for Christians to strengthen their ties to one another, they should not neglect to nurture friendships with people of goodwill outside the churches. In the Czech part of Czechoslovakia, Christian dissidents had to maintain close contact with secular dissidents because there were so few believers within resistance circles.

As lawyer Ján Čarnogurský puts it, "There weren't many people in general who wanted to stand up to communism. You had to take allies where you could. The secret police tried to keep secular liberals and Christians apart, and they wanted to keep Czechs and Slovaks divided. They did not succeed because the leaders of the movement had become friends with leaders in other circles."

In the Slovak region, František Mikloško reached out to liberals not because he had to but because he genuinely wanted to.

"To this day, communicating with the secular liberal world really enriches my views," he says. "It is important for me to have my home and to be aware that I know where I stand. I know my values. But I have to stay in contact with the liberal world, because otherwise there is the danger of degeneration."

Mikloško's close association with secular liberal writers and artists helped him to understand the world beyond church circles and to think critically about himself and other Christian activists. And, he says, liberal artists were able to perceive and describe the essence of communism better than Christians—a skill that helped them all survive, even thrive, under oppression.

In the communist past, secular liberals shared with Christians the conviction that communism was a destructive lie. But today, I put to Mikloško, most liberals seem to think that the kind of oppression coming against religious believers is justified, even necessary, despite its illiberality.

Consider, he says, that good-faith liberals have something to learn from us—and they will only be able to do so if we remain in contact with them.

"I have spent my whole life in the environment of liberals," Mikloško says. "There came a moment in their lives when these people wanted to talk about something deeper. They realized they were seeking, and needed to have somebody to talk to. We Christians have to be present in the world, and be ready when this happens."

Under communism, a well-known liberal intellectual who was known for his atheism quietly asked Mikloško to take him to church. "He told me, 'I tried to pray in my home, but it really didn't work out. He wanted to try in the church. He told me, 'I will try to do whatever you do and see if it works.'"

The Christian activist's point: be kind to others, for you never know when you will need them, or they will need you.

What do you do in a world where you can't be sure who is trustworthy? One response is to withdraw into circles of confidence. Another response—a risky one, it must be said—is not to worry about it, and to be kind anyway.

"Father Jerzy knew that the whole society was infiltrated by communist agents. The priest who was his neighbor was a communist agent. The priest who announced his death right here in the church was a communist agent," says Paweł Kęska, curator of the Popiełuszko museum. "But Father Jerzy said one important thing: 'You can't worry about who's an agent and who's not an agent. If you do, you will tear yourself apart as a community.'"

Kęska tells a story about a stranger who came to Father Jerzy to bring him a package. He ended up staying with Father Jerzy for three years, until his death. He was an atheist, but over time, came to be interested in the faith. Once he asked Father Jerzy something about the Bible. Father Jerzy answered him but kept the focus on the man as a human being, not a potential convert.

"When it comes to survival, maybe what's most important is simple fidelity: not by evangelizing people directly but by developing honest relations with one another—not looking for whether one is good or bad, or judging them by their ideology," says Kęska. "He was constantly observed by the secret police, parked right in front of his home. During the severely cold winters, he would bring them hot tea to warm them up. Because they were people, just like that."

Making Grief Easier to Carry

Vakhtang Mikeladze is a well-known documentary filmmaker from the country of Georgia. He is advanced in age, but still filled with theatrical, old-world flair. Visiting him in his Moscow apartment involves raising more than a few glasses of Georgian brandy in sentimental toasts. It also takes an American visitor into a world of almost incomprehensible suffering.

Mikeladze's father, Evgeni, was a famous orchestral conductor in Tbilisi when he somehow ran afoul of Stalin. In 1937, he was arrested, tortured, and shot by the NKVD, the predecessor of the KGB. Vakhtang, then fifteen, and his seventeen-year-old sister were taken into custody under a law that mandated punishment for family members of "traitors to the fatherland."

During our long, emotional conversation, Vakhtang spoke of the shame he carries with him still, but he did not reveal why until the end when, in tears, he told me about the night the secret police came for the Mikeladze teens.

"When they arrested my sister and me, we were completely scared," he says. "They put us in the back of a truck. They put my aunt in the cab, with a soldier. When they went out of the building into the truck, they had this kind of closed courtyard. Everyone was out there watching and weeping.

"As we drove, my sister and I were sitting across from each

other looking at one another. There was a soldier on either side of us. As we were driving along, out of nowhere different trucks were joining us on the highway. We became a long caravan of the arrested. When we realized all these other trucks were full of the arrested, she looked at me and smiled, and I smiled back. We realized that at least we weren't alone."

The tears flow freely now. The old man softly mutters, "I'm ashamed that I was glad at that moment."

As painful as that memory is for Mikeladze, who would go on to spend many years in the gulag, it testifies to the importance of camaraderie amid travail. Father Kirill Kaleda tells a story about Saint Alexei Mechev, a Moscow priest who died in 1923. Earlier in his life, Father Alexei's wife died of an illness, leaving him with six children to raise. Bereft and paralyzed, Father Alexei sought the advice of Father John of Kronstadt, a well-known Russian Orthodox priest who was canonized after his death in 1909. Father John told the mourning priest, "Join your grief with the grief of others, and then you will find it easier to carry."

Father Alexei took the advice. He went on to become a renowned pastor, spiritual father, and counselor of the broken. When he died in 1923, the Bolshevik regime let Tikhon, the patriarch of Moscow, out of prison to celebrate Father Alexei's funeral. Father Alexei's son Sergei also became a priest. In 1944, Father Sergei was executed in prison by the Soviets for his faith. Both father and son are now canonized saints. Their icon sits above the fireplace in my living room.

College instructor Mária Komáromi sees so much loneliness among the students at her Budapest institution. She thinks about the communist years, when she and her late husband held small group meetings with young Christians in their Budapest apartment. Those sessions helped struggling youth so much, she remembers. Maybe something like that could do so again.

"The first step no doubt is to acknowledge this loneliness," she says. "For young people, the fact that they have lots of social media friends conceals the problem. So we have to counteract that loneliness. That can be done by forming small communities around basically anything."

Sir Roger Scruton, who helped Czech allies build the intellectual resistance, emphasizes the importance today of dissidents creating and committing to small groups—not just church communities, but clubs, singing groups, sports societies, and so forth. The point is to find something to draw you out of yourself, to discover your own worth in relation to others, and to learn how to accept the discipline that comes through accountability to others and a shared purpose. Indeed, Václav Benda, though a Christian, worked hard to bring his fellow Czechs of all creeds together for any purpose at all, if only to defy the fear and atomization that the totalitarian regime depended on to carry out its rule.

Komáromi agrees that we have to start somewhere in our rebellion against contemporary atomization. The individual standing alone against the machine will be crushed.

Organize Now, While You Can

Zofia Romaszewska is one of the true heroes of modern Poland. She and her late husband, Zbigniew, were academics and activists in the Solidarity trade-union movement. The couple joined the fight for liberty and human rights in the 1960s, when they hosted

dissident meetings at their apartment. When the communist regime declared martial law in 1980 in an attempt to smash Solidarity, Romaszewska and her husband went into hiding, and founded
the underground Solidarity radio station. She was eventually arrested, but amnestied after several months.

Today, at eighty, Romaszewska, now a grande dame of the anticommunist resistance, still retains the spark and tenacity of a street
fighter. After five minutes of speaking with her in her Warsaw flat,
it's clear that any commissar faced with a firebrand like this woman
would have no chance of prevailing.

Romaszewska is fierce on the subject of, well, solidarity. She
sees the danger of soft totalitarianism coming fast, and urges young
people to get off the internet and get together face-to-face to build
resistance.

"As I see it, this is the core, this is the essence of everything right
now: Forming these communities and networks of communities,"
she says. "Whatever kinds of communities you can imagine. The
point is that the members of that community must be very supportive of one another, no matter what comes. You don't have to be
prepared to give your life for the other person, but you do have to
have something in common, and to do things together."

See, Judge, Act

The atomization of contemporary life has left most of us vulnerable
to demoralization—and therefore, to manipulation. Christians are
no different. It's easy for believers to feel that they are all alone,

180

even when they are gathered at worship. By their indifference to solidarity, and surrendering to social disintegration as the new normal, Christians make it easier for those in power who hate us to control us.

We desperately need to throw off the chains of solitude and find the freedom that awaits us in fellowship. The testimony of anti-communist dissidents is clear: Only in solidarity with others can we find the spiritual and communal strength to resist. The longer we remain isolated in a period of liberty, the harder it will be to find one another in a time of persecution. We must see in our brothers and sisters not a burden of obligation but the blessing of our own freedom from loneliness, suspicion, and defeat.

Discerning the criteria for comradeship is risky business when trusting the wrong person could land you in prison. Some, like Father Jerzy Popiełuszko, remained open to all, but most Christian dissidents learned to be extremely careful. Not only their safety but also the welfare of the entire church movement was at stake. These lines must be drawn according to particular circumstances. As Father Kolaković's example teaches, Christians should educate themselves about the mechanics of running underground cells and networks while they are still free to do so.

Christians must act to build bonds of brotherhood not just with one another, across denominational and international lines, but also with people of goodwill belonging to other religions, and no religion at all. When their souls are rightly ordered, believers serve not only the good of the church, but are a means of God's blessing to all people.

Leaders of small groups must be willing and able to carry out catechetical, ministerial, and organizational roles normally performed by institutional church leaders who may be unable to do so under the law, or are too compromised in other ways to serve their proper function.

Finally, small-group fellowship keeps morale high when the contempt and torment of the world lashes hard the backs of believers. The young Christians in Moscow in the 1970s remember their time together, worshipping and praying and building one another up, as the happiest of their lives. They bent under the weight of the Soviet state, but they did not break, because God was with them—and so were their brothers and sisters in Christ.

If love was the mortar that bound their fellowship, then shared suffering is what activated the bond and made it real. Suffering was the proof test. Love, as Paul tells us, endures all things. And this is the thing about soft totalitarianism: It seduces those—even Christians—who have lost the capacity to love enduringly, for better or for worse. They think they love, but they merely desire. They think they follow Jesus, but in fact, they merely admire him.

Each of us thinks we wouldn't be like that. But if we have accepted the great lie of our therapeutic culture, which tells us that personal happiness is the greatest good of all, then we will surrender at the first sign of trouble.

CHAPTER TEN

The Gift of Suffering

I am riding on a Budapest tram with a Hungarian friend in her early thirties. We are on our way to interview an older woman who endured real persecution in the communist era. As we bump along the city's streets, my friend talks about how hard it is to be honest with friends her age about the struggles she faces as a wife and mother of young children.

Her difficulties are completely ordinary for a young woman learning how to be a mom and a wife—yet the prevailing attitude among her generation is that life's difficulties are a threat to one's well-being, and should be refused. Do she and her husband argue at times? Then she should leave him. Are her children annoying her? Then she should send them to day care. She worries that her friends don't grasp that suffering is a normal part of life—even of part of a good life, in that suffering teaches us how to be patient, kind, and loving. She doesn't want them to give her advice about how to escape her problems; she just wants them to help her live through them.

I tell my friend that this is the argument that John the Savage has with the World Controller near the end of Huxley's *Brave New World*. The Savage, I explain to my friend, is an outcast in a world that sees suffering, even mere unhappiness, as intolerable oppression. He is fighting for his right to be unhappy—"and so," I tell my friend, "are you."

As we step off the tram and walk to our meeting, we talk about the irony of the social about-face that has overtaken postcommunist Hungary. The woman I am about to meet, like all the Christians I had been interviewing, allowed the suffering inflicted by the communist regime to deepen her love for God and for her fellow persecuted believers. Now, in liberty and relative prosperity, the children of the last communist generation have fallen to a more subtle, sophisticated tyranny: one that tells them that anything they find difficult is a form of oppression. For these millennials, unhappiness is slavery and freedom is liberation from the burden of unchosen obligations.

Though these decadent sentiments may be shocking because they have emerged in a postcommunist country, they are by no means limited to young Hungarians. A 2019 NBC News/*Wall Street Journal* poll found a distinct minority of young American adults believed that religion, patriotism, and having children are an important part of life, while nearly four out of five said "self-fulfillment" is key to the good life.[1] Similarly, the sociologist of religion Christian Smith found in his study of that generation that most of them believe society is nothing more than "a collection of autonomous individuals out to enjoy life."

These are the people who would welcome the Pink Police State. This is the generation that would embrace soft totalitarianism. These are the young churchgoers who have little capacity to resist, because they have been taught that the good life is a life free from suffering. If they have been taught the faith at all, it has been a Christianity without tears.

Suffering As Testimony to the Truth

Though again, the totalitarianism we are facing today looks far more like Huxley's than Orwell's, both books teach a lesson about suffering and truth—and so do the survivors who felt the communist lash.

These lessons are important for us to take into our hearts. The days to come are going to force American Christians to confront personal suffering for the faith in ways most never have done before (African American Christians are the obvious exception). Besides, it cannot be emphasized strongly enough: the old totalitarianism conquered societies through fear of pain; the new one will conquer primarily through manipulating people's love of pleasure and fear of discomfort.

We should not conflate being socially or professionally marginalized with prison camps and the executioner's bullet—the latter of which were all too real for anti-communist dissidents. But know this too: if we latter-day believers are not able and willing to be faithful in the relatively small trials we face now, there is no reason to think we will have what it takes to endure serious persecution in the future.

"Without being willing to suffer, even die for Christ, it's just hypocrisy. It's just a search for comfort," says Yuri Sipko, the Russian Baptist pastor. "When I meet with brothers in faith, especially young people, I ask them: name three values as Christians that you are ready to die for. This is where you see the border between those who are serious about their faith and those who aren't."

When he thinks of the communist past, about Christians who were sent to prison camps and never returned, of those who were ridiculed in the world, who lost their jobs, who even in some cases had their children taken from them because of their faith, Sipko knows what gave them the strength to endure. Their ability to suffer all of this for the sake of Christ is what testified to the reality of their unseen God.

"You need to confess him and worship him in such a way that people can see that this world is a lie," says the old pastor. "This is hard, but this is what reveals man as an image of God."

Mária Komáromi teaches in a Catholic school in Budapest. She and her late husband, János, were religious dissidents under the communist regime, and bore many burdens to keep the faith alive.

"You have to suffer for the truth because that's what makes you authentic. That's what makes that truth credible. If I'm not willing to suffer, my truth might as well be nothing more than an ideology," she tells me.

Komáromi elaborates further:

> Suffering is a part of every human's life. We don't know why we suffer. But your suffering is like a seal. If you put that seal on your actions, interestingly enough, people start to wonder about your truth—that maybe you are right about God. In one sense, it's a mystery, because the Evil One wants to persuade us that there is a life without suffer-

ing. First you have to live through it, and then you try to pass on the value of suffering, because suffering has a value.

Wealth, success, and status are no real defenses against suffering, Komáromi says. Look at all the people who have everything this world can offer, but who still fall into self-destructive behavior, even suicide. Christians must embrace suffering because that's what Jesus did, and because they have the promise, on faith, that to share in his suffering will bring glory in the next life. But sometimes, she adds, we can see results in this life.

"When I started to have children, more children came," says Komáromi, whose kids are all adults now. "When we welcomed all these children back then, we were treated as idiots. Now, though, the whole situation has reversed, and people are so envious that we have such a big family. So in the long run, there is a sort of proof."

Mária Wittner, now in her eighties, is regarded by her countrymen as a national hero for fighting the Soviets when they invaded Hungary in 1956. She was only a teenager then. The communist regime arrested her shortly after she turned twenty, and a year later, sentenced her to death. Her sentence was later reduced because of her youth. But she endured terrible grief and pain in her eight months on death row.

"There was an execution either every day or every other day, by hanging," she tells me. "The people who were being brought to the execution, each one said their name aloud and left some sort of message in their final words. Some sang the national anthem, others praised their country, there were people saying, 'Avenge me!'"

There were days when several people were hanged, even seven a day. Wittner's friend Catherine was also sentenced to death. They spent Catherine's last night together in the cell, and said their final goodbyes after sunrise. Wittner explains:

> The guards took her. The last sight I saw of her was that she straightened herself up and went with her back ramrod straight. The door closed, and then I was left alone. I started to bang on the door, shouting, "Bring her back!" even though I knew perfectly well that it wouldn't matter. Then I fainted. When I came to my senses, I swore to myself that I will never be silent about what I have seen, if I have the opportunity to bear witness.

This, she believes, is why her life was spared: so that she could tell the world what the communists did to people like her.

"I've been thinking a lot about fear, as such," she says. "What is fear? Someone who is afraid is going to be made to do the most evil things. If someone is not afraid to say no, if your soul is free, there is nothing they can do to you."

The old woman looks at me across her kitchen table with piercing eyes. "In the end, those who are afraid always end up worse than the courageous."

Admirers or Disciples?

The filmmaker Terrence Malick frames the conflict in his 2019 masterpiece, *A Hidden Life*, perhaps the best cinematic evocation of both the Gospel and the inner drama of resisting totalitarianism as a clash of rival religions: Nazism and Catholicism.

It is based on the true story of Franz Jägerstätter, an Austrian Catholic farmer who refuses to serve in the Nazi army because he will not swear loyalty to Adolf Hitler. For him, that would be an act of idolatry. The Nazis sent Jägerstätter to prison and executed him in 1943 for his treason. In 2007, Pope Benedict XVI beatified him as a martyr.

In the film, nearly all of the peasants in Jägerstätter's tiny Alpine village accept Nazism without protest. Some do so with enthusiasm. Others have private doubts but are too afraid to speak them. Even the parish priest tells Franz that it would be better for his wife and children if he kept his mouth shut and conformed. Franz and his wife, Fani, are the only ones who both understand how evil Nazi totalitarianism is and are willing to suffer for bearing witness to their conviction.

A Hidden Life makes clear that the source of their resistance was their deep Catholic faith. Yet everyone in the village is also Catholic—yet they conform to the Nazi world. Why did the Jägerstätters see, judge, and act as they did, but not one of their fellow Christians?

The answer comes in a conversation Franz has with an old artist who is painting images of Bible stories on the wall of the village church. The artist laments his own inability to truly represent Christ. His images comfort believers, but they do not lead them to repentance and conversion. Says the painter, "We create admirers. We do not create followers."

Malick, who wrote the screenplay and who was trained in philosophy, almost certainly draws that distinction from the nineteenth-century Christian existentialist Søren Kierkegaard, who wrote Jesus didn't proclaim a philosophy, but a way of life.

Christ understood that being a "disciple" was in innermost and deepest harmony with what he said about himself. Christ claimed to be the way and the truth and the life (Jn. 14:6). For this reason, he could never be satisfied with adherents who accepted his teaching—especially with those who in their lives ignored it or let things take their usual course. His whole life on earth, from beginning to end, was destined solely to have followers and to make admirers impossible.[2]

Admirers love being associated with Jesus, but when trouble comes, they either turn on him or in some way try to put distance between themselves and the Lord. The admirer wants the comfort and advantage that comes with being a Christian, but when times change and Jesus becomes a scandal or worse, the admirer folds. As Kierkegaard writes:

> The admirer never makes any true sacrifices. He always plays it safe. Though in words, phrases, songs, he is inexhaustible about how highly he prizes Christ, he renounces nothing, will not reconstruct his life, and will not let his life express what it is he supposedly admires. Not so for the follower. No, no. The follower aspires with all his strength to be what he admires. And then, remarkably enough, even though he is living amongst a "Christian people," he incurs the same peril as he did when it was dangerous to openly confess Christ.[3]

The follower recognizes the cost of discipleship and is willing to pay it. This does not mean that he is obligated to put himself at maximum peril at all times, or stand guilty of being an admirer. But it does mean that when the Gestapo or the KGB shows up in his village and demands that he bow to the swastika or the hammer and sickle, the follower will make the sign of the cross and walk with fear and trembling toward Golgotha.

Suffer Without Bitterness

Here is one of Christ's hardest commands:

> But I say unto you, Love your enemies, bless them that curse you, do good to them that hate you, and pray for them which despitefully use you, and persecute you. (Matthew 5:44, KJV)

Many of us find it difficult to be charitable to a sales clerk who is rude to us, or to someone who cuts us off in traffic. Few of us would be able to love someone responsible for us losing our job, or worse, being blacklisted in our profession. Rare is the man or woman who could find love in their hearts for their mugger or rapist.

But then, most of us aren't Silvester Krčméry.

You will recall that Krčméry, who died in 2013, was one of the most important figures in the Slovak Catholic anti-communist resistance. In his eventual court trial, communist prosecutors called him a liar for saying that Czechoslovaks had no religious freedom. *You are allowed to go to church to worship, aren't you?* they taunted—a barb that contemporary US progressives toss at conservatives who argue for religious liberty.

Krčméry threw the accusation back in their faces. He said Jesus is not satisfied with mere churchgoing, but wants believers to live for Christ in all times and places. This is what Krčméry had learned studying with Father Kolaković, and this is what first brought him to the attention of the secret police.

"Do not be afraid and always act as you think Christ would act in your place and in a particular situation," Father Kolaković had taught his followers. When the secret police arrested Krčméry, he laughed, because he understood that he was being given the gift of suffering for Jesus.

In prison, Krčméry was denied a Bible and found himself grateful that he had spent the past few years of freedom memorizing Scripture. Like other political prisoners, Krčméry endured repeated tortures. He had been trained to resist brainwashing. In the end, he relied on faith alone to guide his path. The more he surrendered in his weakness, the greater his spiritual strength.

The young doctor decided to be united in his suffering with Christ's, and to offer his pain as a gift to God for the sake of other persecuted people. He believed that the Lord was allowing him to endure this trial for a reason—but he had to convince himself in the face of his agonies.

"Therefore I repeated again and again: 'I am really God's probe, God's laboratory. I'm going through all this so I can help others, and the Church.'"[4]

Krčméry decided that he had to be useful. He discovered that simple acts of solidarity with fellow sufferers, both given and received, mattered more than he could have imagined. In that communist prison, the biblical command to bear one another's burdens became intensely real. "A brother who helped in hard times was closer in suffering than the closest relatives and friends, outside, often on a permanent basis," he writes. This Catholic layman lived out the truth of the Orthodox priest John of Kronstadt's advice to the widowed priest Alexei Mechev: to join his grief with the griefs of others, and he would find them easier to bear.

Torture, deprivation, isolation—all of those things could have destroyed Silvo Krčméry, and made him a hateful man, or at least a defeated one. But the transcript of his 1954 trial shows that it refined him, purified him, made him strong in the Lord. In his final defense statement, Krčméry defiantly proclaimed to the court:

> God gave me everything I have and now that I face perse-
> cution because of Him, and am called on to profess my
> faith in Him, should I now pretend I don't believe? Should
> I hide my faith? Should I deny Him?[5]

He taunted his communist persecutors, declaring, "We will not allow ourselves to be led to hate, to rebel, or even to complain. . . . That is where our strength and superiority lie."

It would be ten years before Silvester Krčméry saw the outside of a prison. He spent the rest of his life evangelizing from his home in Bratislava and working with the sick, especially addicts. The man who said that refusing hatred was the strength of persecuted Christians did not seek vengeance, even after communism's fall.

"Bless You, Prison": Receive Suffering As a Gift

"Bless those who persecute you," Jesus taught. Vengeance is easier to resist if you have that mind-set. In his masterwork, *The Gulag*

Archipelago, Aleksandr Solzhenitsyn reveals how he and his fellow inmates were beaten, humiliated, deprived of liberty, made to live in filth and freezing temperatures and crawling with lice, and to endure many other grotesque manifestations of communism's determination to create heaven on earth. That's why nothing in that epochal book's pages shocks more than these lines:

> And that is why I turn back to the years of my imprisonment and say, sometimes to the astonishment of those about me: "Bless you, prison! . . . Bless you, prison, for having been in my life!"[6]

Solzhenitsyn's audacious claim was that suffering had refined him, taught him to love. It was only there, out of the experience of intense suffering, that the prisoner began to understand the meaning of life and first began to sense the good inside himself.

To be clear, there is nothing in the Gospels that requires Christians to seek out suffering. The Word of God is not a prescription for masochism. But the life of Christ, as well as the Old Testament's example of the prophets, compels believers to accept the impenetrable mystery that suffering, if rightly received, can be a gift.

Father Kirill Kaleda, the Russian Orthodox priest who pastors the church dedicated to the martyrs of the Bolshevik persecution, offers a prudent view on suffering in the life of a Christian.

"Taking up your cross and carrying it is always going to be uncomfortable. We can say clearly that this current ideology of comfort is anti-Christian in its very essence," says Father Kirill. "But we should point out the fact that the church, not once, ever called its followers to look for suffering, and even made it clear that they are warned not to do that. But if a person finds himself in a situation where he's suffering, then he should bear it with courage."

Alexander Ogorodnikov, whom you met in earlier chapters, is one of the most famous dissidents of the late Soviet period. Born into a communist family, he was a leader in the Komsomol youth movement, his enthusiasm earning him notice from the KGB as a potential recruit. But he converted to Christianity in his twenties. His campaigning for religious liberty landed him a prison sentence in 1978. He was freed nine years later after US president Ronald Reagan and British prime minister Margaret Thatcher appealed to Soviet leader Mikhail Gorbachev on his behalf.

Ogorodnikov, now nearly seventy, is quiet and intense. His face is partially paralyzed as a result of the beatings he received in the gulag. It is one thing to read about the torture of Soviet prison camps in a book. It is quite another to listen to an account from the mouth of a man who experienced it. I find out later from my translator that Ogorodnikov had been anxious about meeting me at my hotel, the Hotel Metropol, because in communist times, it was a KGB den.

Though he did not have a death sentence, Soviet authorities nevertheless decided to teach Ogorodnikov a lesson by placing him on death row in one of the USSR's harshest prisons—a facility where, according to one of Ogorodnikov's captors, the state sent people to be broken, "to bleed you out, drop by drop."

"When I went into the cell and looked at the others who were there, I told them, 'Listen brothers, I was sent here to help you meet death, not as criminals but as men with souls that are going to meet their makers, to go meet God the Father," he tells me. "Given that they always took people to go be shot really early in the morning, many of them didn't sleep. They were waiting for the knock at the door to see who would be called out. So, of course they didn't sleep. Neither did I. I helped them turn this night of terror into a night of hope."

The young Christian, not yet thirty, told these hardened criminals that though he was not a priest, he would still be willing to hear their confessions.

"I told them I couldn't absolve them, but when I die and go before the Lord, I will be a witness to their repentance," he says. "If I wanted to describe for you their confessions, I would need to be Dostoevsky. I don't have the words myself. I told them that God is merciful, and the fact that they are admitting what they had done, and denouncing it, would wash them and purify them. They were all going to be shot sooner or later, but at least they would die with a clean conscience."

When the prison authorities realized that confinement in a cell with the worst of the worst was not leading Ogorodnikov to repent of his sins against the Soviet state, they put him in solitary confinement.

"I was alone in the chamber one night," he remembers. "I felt very clearly that someone woke me up in the middle of the night. It was soft, but clear.

He goes on:

When I woke up, I had a very, very clear vision. I could see the corridor of the jail. I could see the person being taken out of his cell in chains, but I only saw them from behind, but I knew exactly who it was. I understood that

God sent me an angel to wake me up so I could accompany that man in prayer as he was being taken out to be shot.

"Who am I to be shown this?" I asked God. Then I understood that I was seeing the extent of God's love. I understood that the prayers of this prisoner and I had been heard and that he was forgiven. I was in tears. This awakening didn't occur with all of those prisoners, only with some of them.

Ogorodnikov interpreted this as a sign that not all of the prisoners with whom he prayed had been sincere in their repentance. As he languished in solitary confinement, the mystical awakenings continued, as an unseen force would nudge him out of sleep with a gentle touch. The same kind of vision played out in front of the prisoner's open eyes: the image of guards leading a shackled prisoner to his execution.

After this happened a few times, Ogorodnikov wondered why, in these waking visions, he was not allowed to see the condemned prisoners' faces. He did not penetrate this mystery until later, in a different prison, through what he regards as a divine revelation.

In that small prison, Ogorodnikov was the only captive, and he was looked after by a single guard, who was clearly a pensioner, allowed to work the night shift because he was lonely.

One night, he entered Ogorodnikov's cell with a wild look on his face. "They come at night," said the old man to the prisoner. Strange words, but Ogorodnikov understood that the old man was being driven to the brink of insanity by something and that he needed to confess. Ogorodnikov urged him to speak. This is what the haunted prison guard said:

> When I was a young guard in a different prison, they would gather twenty or thirty priests who had been behind bars, and took them outside. They rigged them up to a sled, so that they were pulling the sled. They had them pull the sled out into the forest. They made them run all day, until they brought them to a swamp. And then they put them into two rows, one behind the other. I was one of the guards who stood in the perimeter around the prisoners.
>
> "One of the KGB guys walked up to the first priest. He asked him very calmly and quietly, "Is there a God?" The priest said yes. They shot him in the forehead in such a way that his brains covered the priest standing behind him. He calmly loaded his pistol, went to next priest, and asked, "Does God exist?"
>
> "Yes, he exists." The KGB man shot this priest in the same way. We didn't blindfold them. They saw everything that was about to happen to them.

Ogorodnikov fights back tears as he comes to the end of his story. In a voice cracking with emotion, the old prisoner says, "Not one of those priests denied Christ."

This is why the old man volunteered to keep Ogorodnikov company after sundown: memories of the priests' faces in the moments before their execution haunted him at night. This encounter with the broken prison guard made Ogorodnikov understand why, in his mystical visions, he had not been able to see the faces of the condemned. He too would have been driven mad by the horror. He had to be content with the knowledge that because he had been present to share the Gospel with them, those poor souls, damned in this life, would live forever in paradise.

Expect the Worst, Show Mercy to the Broken

Unless you have been through the experience, it is hard to grasp how mentally fragile torture and solitary confinement can make a man. In *The Gulag Archipelago*, Solzhenitsyn urges his readers to have mercy on prisoners who broke under torture. Nearly all of them did, at some point, he says. Unless you've endured it, he writes, you cannot imagine how great the pressure is to say anything that will make the physical and psychological pain stop.

In his life as a political prisoner in communist Romania, the late Lutheran pastor Richard Wurmbrand testified to both truths. The Romania that Soviet troops occupied at the end of World War II was a deeply religious country. After Romanian Stalinists seized dictatorial control in 1947, among the most vicious anti-Christian persecution in the history of Soviet-style communism began.

From 1949 to 1951, the state conducted the "Piteşti Experiment." The Piteşti prison was established as a factory to reengineer the human soul. Its masters subjected political prisoners, including clergy, to insane methods of torture to utterly destroy them psychologically so they could be remade as fully obedient citizens of the People's Republic.

Wurmbrand, held captive from 1948 until he was ransomed into Western exile in 1964, was an inmate at Piteşti. In 1966 testimony before a US Senate committee, Wurmbrand spoke of how the communists broke bones, used red-hot irons, and all manner of physical torture. They were also spiritually and psychologically sadistic, almost beyond comprehension. Wurmbrand told the story of a young Christian prisoner in Piteşti who was tied to a cross for days. Twice daily, the cross bearing the man was laid flat on the floor, and one hundred other inmates were forced by guards to urinate and defecate on him.

> Then the cross was erected again and the Communists, swearing and mocking, "Look your Christ, look your Christ, how beautiful he is, adore him, kneel before him, how fine he smells, your Christ." And then the Sunday morning came and a Catholic priest, an acquaintance of mine, had been put to the belt, in the dirt of a cell with 100 prisoners, a plate with excrement, and one with urine was given to him and he was obliged to say the holy mass upon these elements, and he did it.[7]

Wurmbrand asked the priest how he could consent to commit such sacrilege. The Catholic priest was "half-mad," Wurmbrand recalled, and begged him to show mercy. All the other prisoners were beaten until they accepted this profane communion while the communist prison guards taunted them.

Wurmbrand told the American lawmakers:

> I am a very insignificant and a very little man. I have been in prison among the weak ones and the little ones, but I speak for a suffering country and for a suffering church and for the heroes and the saints of the twentieth century;

we have had such saints in our prison to which I did not dare to lift my eyes.[8]

After his release, Pastor Wurmbrand, who died in 2001, devoted the rest of his life to speaking out for persecuted Christians. "Not all of us are called to die a martyr's death," he wrote, "but all of us are called to have the same spirit of self-sacrifice and love to the very end as these martyrs had."[9]

Let the Weakness of Others Make You Stronger

Accompanying other persecuted people in their suffering can lead us to deep repentance and spiritual strength. One of Wurmbrand's fellow Piteşti prisoners was George Calciu, an Orthodox Christian medical student who was eventually ordained a priest. In 1985, he was sent into exile in the United States, where he served at a northern Virginia parish until his death in 2006.

In a lengthy 1996 interview, Father George told about his encounter with a fellow prisoner named Constantine Oprisan. They met when Calciu was transferred from Piteşti to Jilava, a prison that was built entirely underground. The communists put four prisoners in each cell. In his cell was Oprisan, who was deathly ill with tuberculosis. From their first day in captivity there, Oprisan coughed up fluid in his lungs.

The man was suffocating. Perhaps a whole liter of phlegm and blood came up, and my stomach became upset. I was ready to vomit. Constantine Oprisan noticed this and said to me, "Forgive me." I was so ashamed! Since I was a student in medicine, I decided then to take care of him . . . and told the others that I would take care of Constantine Oprisan. He was not able to move, and I did everything for him. I put him on the bucket to urinate. I washed his body. I fed him. We had a bowl for food. I took this bowl and put it in front of his mouth.[10]

Constantine Oprisan—"he was like a saint," Father George said—was so weak that he could barely talk. But every word he said to his cellmates was about Christ. Hearing him say his daily prayers had a profound effect on the other three men, as did simply looking at the "flood of love in his face."

Constantine Oprisan was a physical wreck because he had been so badly tortured in Pitești for three years, reported Father George. Yet he would not curse his torturers and spent his days in prayer.

All the while, we did not realize how important Constantine Oprisan was for us. He was the justification of our life in this cell. Over the course of a year, he became weaker and weaker. We felt that he had finished his time here and would die.[11]

After he died

every one of us felt that something in us had died. We understood that, sick as he was and in our care like a child, he had been the pillar of our life in the cell.[12]

After the cellmates washed his body and prepared it for burial, they alerted the guards that Constantine Oprisan was dead. The guards led the men out of the windowless cell for the first time in a year. Then one guard ordered Calciu and another man to take the body outside and bury it. Constantine Oprisan was nothing but skin and bones; his muscle tissue had wasted away. For some reason, the skin pulled tight over his emaciated skeleton had turned yellow.

> My friend took a flower and put it on his chest—a blue flower. The guard started to cry out to us and forced us to go back into the cell. Before we went into the cell, we turned around and looked at Constantine Oprisan—his yellow body and this blue flower. This is the image that I have kept in my memory—the body of Constantine Oprisan completely emaciated and the blue flower on his chest.[13]

Looking back on that drama nearly a half century later, Father George said that nursing the helpless Constantine Oprisan in the final year of his life revealed to him "the light of God."

> When I took care of Constantine Oprisan in the cell, I was very happy. I was very happy because I felt his spirituality penetrating my soul. I learned from him to be good, to forgive, not to curse your torturer, not to consider anything of this world to be a treasure for you. In fact, he was living on another level. Only his body was with us—and his love. Can you imagine? We were in a cell without windows, without air, humid, filthy—yet we had moments of

happiness that we never reached in freedom. I cannot explain it.[14]

In terms of sacramental theology, a mystery is a truth that cannot be explained, only accepted. The long death of Constantine
Oprisan, which gave spiritual life to those who helped him bear his
suffering, is just such a mystery. The stricken prisoner was dying,
but because he had already died to himself for Christ's sake, he was
able to be an icon to the others—a window into eternity through
which the divine light passed to illuminate the other men in that
dark, filthy cell.

A Christianity for the Days to Come

The faith of martyrs, and confessors like those who survived to bear
witness, is a far cry from the therapeutic religion of the middle-
class suburbs, the sermonizing of politicized congregations of the
Left and the Right, and the health-and-wealth message of "prosperity gospel" churches. These and other feeble forms of the faith
will be quickly burned away in the face of the slightest persecution.
Pastor Wurmbrand once wrote that there were two kinds of Christians: "those who sincerely believe in God and those who, just as
sincerely, believe that they believe. You can tell them apart by their
actions in decisive moments."[15]

The kind of Christians we will be in the time of testing depends
on the kind of Christians we are today. And we cannot become the
kind of Christians we need to be in preparation for persecution if
we don't know stories like this, and take them into our hearts.

I shared some of these accounts with a Czech friend who left his communist homeland for America in his twenties. This kind of story is not news to him—and yet, he wrote, "It's difficult to read. It's even more difficult to realize that it has been nearly forgotten, or worse, never known."

See, Judge, Act

To recognize the value in suffering is to rediscover a core teaching of historical Christianity, and to see clearly the pilgrim path walked by every generation of Christians since the Twelve Apostles. There is nothing more important than this when building up Christian resistance to the coming totalitarianism. It is also to declare oneself a kind of savage in today's culture—even within the culture of the church. It requires standing foursquare against much of popular Christianity, which has become a shallow self-help cult whose chief aim is not cultivating discipleship but rooting out personal anxieties. But to refuse to see suffering as a means of sanctification is to surrender, in Huxley's withering phrase, to "Christianity without tears."

How are we supposed to judge the right approach to suffering though? Unfortunately, there is no clear formula. As Father Kirill Kaleda says, we ought not to go out looking for it. Even Christ, in Gethsemane, prayed that the cup of suffering might be taken from him if it be God's will. The virtue of prudence is critical, in part to help us discern the difference between reasoning and rationalizing. All of us prefer the cup to pass, but if our moment comes, then we have to be ready to make a costly stand.

We will not know how to behave when that time arrives if we have not prepared ourselves to accept pain and loss for the sake of God's kingdom. Most of us in the West don't yet have opportunities to suffer for the faith like Christians under communism did, but we have their stories to guide us, as well as the accounts of Christian martyrdom worldwide throughout the ages. Familiarize yourself with their stories, and teach them to your children. These stories are near the core of the lived Christian experience, and form an essential part of Christian cultural memory. Learn them, so you will know when and how to live them.

God cannot will evil, though as he showed in his Passion, he can permit suffering for some greater good. Judging accurately whether or not he is calling us to share in his Passion in a particular instance requires having faith that our suffering will have purpose, though that purpose may not be clear to us at the time. When he went to prison as a layman, George Calciu was moved to deep conversion by the witness of priests who were his fellow inmates. When he returned to prison later in life, Calciu was a priest and led other inmates to Christ as he had been led decades earlier. Ogorodnikov's ministry, he is confident, led condemned men to paradise. Krčméry's laid the groundwork for the underground church. Solzhenitsyn emerged from the grinding misery of the gulag as a fearless man of God whose prophetic witness to the world helped bring down an evil empire.

When we act—either to embrace suffering on our own or to share in the suffering of others—we have to let it change us, as it changed these confessors of the communist yoke. It could make us bitter, angry, and vengeful, or it could serve as a refiner's fire, as it did with Solzhenitsyn, Calciu, Krčméry, Ogorodnikov, and so many others, purifying our love of God and tortured humanity.

No Christian has the power to avoid suffering entirely. It is the human condition. What we do control is how we act in the face of it. Will we run from it and betray our Lord? Or will we accept it as a severe mercy? The choices we will make when put to the ultimate test depend on the choices we make today, in a time of peace. This is what Father Tomislav Kolaković understood when he arrived in Czechoslovakia and set about preparing the church for the coming persecution. This is why when the secret police came for Silvester Krčméry, he knew how to carry that cross like a true Christian.

CONCLUSION

Live Not by Lies

---

*Father Kolaković saw what was coming and prepared
Christians for it. Don't doubt it. He is speaking to us even
now. He is telling us what to do.*

**DR. NICHOLAS BARTULICA, 92,
A CROATIAN ÉMIGRÉ AND KOLAKOVIĆ FRIEND**

W hat if the answers to life's questions that young Christians the world over are looking for are not to be found
in the West but rather in the East—in the stories and
lives of the Christian dissidents? That's what one young Slovak
man learned, to his great surprise, when he began reporting on a
project about the persecuted Christians of the communist era.

Though he was only a toddler when the Velvet Revolution
ended totalitarianism in his country, Timo Križka knows about

the suffering of Christians under communism better than most. The Bratislava photographer and filmmaker's great-grandfather, a Greek Catholic priest, was forced out of ministry in the 1950s for refusing the government's order to convert to the Orthodox Church, which at that time was under Soviet control. That priest, Father Michal Durišin, chose a life of suffering for himself and his family, rather than stain his conscience.

Several years ago, Križka set out to honor his ancestor's sacrifice by interviewing and photographing the still-living Slovak survivors of communist persecution, including original members of Father Kolaković's fellowship, the Family. As he made his rounds around his country, Križka was shaken up not by the stories of suffering he heard—these he expected—but by the intense inner peace radiating from these elderly believers.

These men and women had been around Križka's age when they had everything taken from them but their faith in God. And yet, over and over, they told their young visitor that in prison they found inner liberation through suffering. One Christian, separated from his wife and five children and cast into solitary confinement, testified that he had moments then that were "like paradise."

"It seemed that the less they were able to change the world around them, the stronger they had become," Križka tells me. "These people completely changed my understanding of freedom. My project changed from looking for victims to finding heroes. I stopped building a monument to the unjust past. I began to look for a message for us, the free people."

The message he found was this: The secular liberal ideal of freedom so popular in the West, and among many in his postcommunist generation, is a lie. That is, the concept that real freedom is found by liberating the self from all binding commitments (to God, to marriage, to family), and by increasing worldly comforts—that is a road that leads to hell. Križka observed that the only force in society standing in the middle of that wide road yelling "Stop!" were the traditional Christian churches.

And then it hit him.

"With our eyes fixed intently on the West, we could see how it was beginning to experience the same things we knew from the time of totalitarianism," he tells me. "Once again, we are all being told that Christian values stand in the way of the people having a better life. History has already shown us how far this kind of thing can go. We also know what to do now, in terms of making life decisions."

From his interviews with former Christian prisoners, Križka also learned something important about himself. He had always thought that suffering was something to be escaped. Yet he never understood why the easier and freer his professional and personal life became, his happiness did not commensurately increase. His generation was the first one since the Second World War to know liberty—so why did he feel so anxious and never satisfied?

These meetings with elderly dissidents revealed a life-giving truth to the seeker. It was the same truth it took Aleksandr Solzhenitsyn a tour through the hell of the Soviet gulag to learn.

"Accepting suffering is the beginning of our liberation," he says. "Suffering can be the source of great strength. It gives us the power to resist. It is a gift from God that invites us to change. To start a revolution against the oppression. But for me, the oppressor was no longer the totalitarian communist regime. It's not even the progressive liberal state. Meeting these hidden heroes started a revolution against the greatest totalitarian ruler of all: myself."

Križka discovered a subtle but immensely important truth: We ourselves are the ultimate rulers of our consciences. Hard totalitarianism depends on terrorizing us into surrendering our free consciences; soft totalitarianism uses fear as well, but mostly it bewitches us with therapeutic promises of entertainment, pleasure, and comfort—including, in the phrase of Mustapha Mond, Huxley's great dictator, "Christianity without tears."

But truth cannot be separated from tears. To live in truth requires accepting suffering. In *Brave New World*, Mond appeals to John the Savage to leave his wild life in the woods and return to the comforts of civilization. The prophetic savage refuses the temptation.

> "But I don't want comfort. I want God, I want poetry, I want real danger, I want freedom, I want goodness. I want sin."
>
> "In fact," said Mustapha Mond, "you're claiming the right to be unhappy."
>
> "All right then," said the Savage defiantly, "I'm claiming the right to be unhappy."[1]

This is the cost of liberty. This is what it means to live in truth. There is no other way. There is no escape from the struggle. The price of liberty is eternal vigilance—first of all, over our own hearts.

God's Saboteurs

"Modern history teaches us that the fight for freedom is always with us," says Marek Benda, who fought the communist regime as a teenager alongside his mother and father. "A single generation always stands between us and tyranny. Many people can look back and see the lessons of history, but they are totally blind to the danger that these same things are happening now."

I hope that reading the testimonies of the men and women in this book has caused the scales to fall from your eyes. But as Father Tomislav Kolaković taught his disciples as the shadow of Soviet totalitarianism grew long over their land, seeing is only the first step. Think about what you see. Get together with others to talk about what you are all seeing. Analyze the facts and discern how your faith and your moral convictions should be applied concretely to the situation.

Then act—while there is still time. As C. S. Lewis put it, the world is "enemy-occupied territory" for the Christian. "Christianity is the story of how the rightful king has landed, you might say landed in disguise, and is calling us all to take part in a great campaign of sabotage." The culture war is largely over—and we lost. The Grand March is, for the time being, a victory parade. But then, so were the May Day marches and pageants in all the cities and towns of the late Soviet Empire.

The Marxist Mordor was real, but the faith of those who resisted outlasted it, because hard totalitarianism met something harder: the truth. In our time, the emerging totalitarianism is softer, smarter, and more sophisticated—but is no less totalitarian for it. Lubomir Gleiman, who listened to Father Kolaković's Bratislava lectures in 1943, wrote in his 2006 memoir that Kolaković believed communism "was more ruthless than the Western secularized 'soft' totalitarianism," and therefore the greater threat to Christianity at the time.[2] But as Timo Križka, a son of the first generation of post-Soviet freedom, discovered, the totalitarianism that Father Kolaković identified as soft really exists. Like its more brutal older brother, it is built on the oldest lie of all, the one the serpent whispered in the Garden, the father of every other lie: "Ye shall be as gods."

Our cause appears lost . . . but we are still here! Now our mission is to build the underground resistance to the occupation to keep alive the memory of who we were and who we are, and to stoke the fires of desire for the true God. Where there is memory and desire, there is hope. Let all saboteurs for the Kingdom of God heed the stirring conclusion of Aleksandr Solzhenitsyn's 1974 essay, "Live Not by Lies!," which gives this book its title. It was his valedictory to the Russian people:

> And so: We need not be the first to set out on this path, Ours is but to join! The more of us set out together, the thicker our ranks, the easier and shorter will this path be for us all! If we become thousands—they will not cope, they will be unable to touch us. If we will grow to tens of thousands—we will not recognize our country!
>
> But if we shrink away, then let us cease complaining that someone does not let us draw breath—we do it to ourselves! Let us then cower and hunker down, while our comrades the biologists bring closer the day when our thoughts can be read and our genes altered.
>
> And if from this also we shrink away, then we are worthless, hopeless, and it is of us that Pushkin asks with scorn:
>
> Why should cattle have the gifts of freedom?
>
> Their heritage from generation to generation is the belled yoke and the lash.[3]

ACKNOWLEDGMENTS

I am not at liberty to thank some of those who helped me research this book, because it would put them at risk of retaliation in the workplace. None of these anonymous helpers live in the former Soviet Bloc; all are Americans. That tells us something important. But you know who you are, and I thank you.

This book exists because of Dr. John Schirger and his mother, Milada Kloubkova Schirger. It was she, a former Catholic prisoner of conscience in her native Czechoslovakia, who said to her US-born son that she was seeing things happening in America that reminded her of her own homeland under communism. Dr. Schirger passed his mother's remarks on to me in 2015, but at the time he preferred to keep their identity private. His mother's story was the genesis of *Live Not by Lies*. Milada Schirger died in 2019, at the age of ninety-two. In gratitude for her witness, her son gave me permission to identify them both. I hope this book is worthy of her legacy.

My friends Béla and Gabriella Bollobás, who fled Hungary for freedom in Britain in the 1960s, first confirmed to me that I should take Milada Schirger seriously. This book is theirs too. I am grateful for all I have learned from them over the years.

I want to thank the translators and guides who helped me overseas. Father Štěpán Smolen was my Virgil in the Czech Republic, with the help of Milan Žonca and Andrej Kutarna. Łukasz Kożuchowski was my right hand in Warsaw; in the Romaszewska interview there, I was also assisted by Aneta Wisniewska and Wojciech Kolarski. Matthew Casserly aided me in Moscow. Anna Salyi was my Budapest fixer and translator. Viliam Ostatník was my able assistant in Bratislava.

I had other invaluable help setting up meetings with remarkable men and women. In Russia, I could not have done this work without the aid of Dmitry Uzlaner; I cannot thank him enough. In Slovakia, Juraj Šúst and Timo Križka introduced me to the world of the Slovak Catholic underground. Ryszard Legutko and Dariusz Karłowicz were key to my work in Poland. In fact, Ryszard's great book *The Demon in Democracy* is an invaluable guide to understanding the soft totalitarianism of our time.

Once again, I have the opportunity to express gratitude to my literary agent, Gary Morris of the David Black Agency, who, for the nearly two decades he has been in my life, has been everything a writer could hope for. This is the second book I have done with Bria Sandford, my editor at Sentinel. I appreciate her confidence in me and my ideas. I also owe a debt of thanks to my friend Dewey Scandurro, for his prayers and advice on the drafts of this book, as he has offered during the writing of almost all of my books.

Thanks also to my wife, Julie, and children, Matthew, Lucas, and Nora, for their patience during my lengthy absences reporting this book. Kids, these stories are for you and your generation more than for your mother's and mine.

ACKNOWLEDGMENTS

Finally I want to thank Frederica Mathewes-Green, one of my oldest and dearest friends. Her spiritual father was the Orthodox priest George Calciu, which is how I first learned of him and of the torture camp at Piteşti, in Romania. For over twenty-five years, Frederica has supported me with her friendship, her wise counsel, and through her willingness to listen to me and pray for me through my struggles, in particular with this project.

NOTES

INTRODUCTION

1. Aleksandr Solzhenitsyn, *The Gulag Archipelago 1918–1956*, trans. Thomas P. Whitney and Harry Willetts; abr. by Edward E. Ericson Jr. (NY: Perennial, 1983). Quote taken from the author's introduction to the abridgment (no page number).
2. "In New Biography, Pope Benedict XVI Laments Modern 'Anti-Christian Creed,'" *National Catholic Register*, May 4, 2020, ncregister.com/daily-news/in-new-biography-pope-benedict-xvi-laments-modern-anti-christian-creed.
3. Aleksandr Solzhenitsyn, "Live Not by Lies!," in *The Solzhenitsyn Reader: New and Selected Writings, 1947–2005*, eds. Edward E. Ericson Jr. and Daniel J. Mahoney (Wilmington, DE: ISI Books, 2009), 558.

CHAPTER ONE: KOLAKOVIĆ THE PROPHET

1. Václav Vaško, "Professor Kolaković: Myths and Reality," trans. Google, *Impulz* no. 3 (2006), impulzrevue.sk/article.php?135.

2. Hannah Arendt, *The Origins of Totalitarianism* (NY: Harcourt, 1973), viii.

3. Czesław Miłosz, *The Captive Mind* (NY: Vintage, 1990), 6.

4. René Girard, *I Saw Satan Fall Like Lightning*, trans. James G. Williams (NY: Orbis, 2001), 179.

5. George Orwell, *Nineteen Eighty-Four* (NY: Houghton Mifflin Harcourt, 1983), 62.

6. Orwell, *Nineteen Eighty-Four*, 62.

7. Miłosz, *Captive Mind*, 5.

8. Miłosz, *Captive Mind*, 73.

9. Aleksandr Solzhenitsyn, "Live Not by Lies!," in *The Solzhenitsyn Reader: New and Selected Writings, 1947–2005*, eds. Edward E. Ericson Jr. and Daniel J. Mahoney (Wilmington, DE: ISI Books, 2009), 556.

10. Solzhenitsyn, "Lies!," 559.

CHAPTER TWO: OUR PRE-TOTALITARIAN CULTURE

1. Nadine Gordimer, *Telling Times: Writing and Living, 1950–2008* (London: Bloomsbury, 2010), 474.

2. Aleksandr Solzhenitsyn, *The Gulag Archipelago 1918–1956*, trans. Thomas P. Whitney and Harry Willetts; abr. by Edward E. Ericson Jr. (NY: Perennial, 1983), 39.

3. Yuri Slezkine, *The House of Government: A Saga of the Russian Revolution* (Princeton, NJ: Princeton University Press, 2019), 36–37.

4. Slezkine, *House of Government*, 40.

5. Anne Applebaum, *Iron Curtain: The Crushing of Eastern Europe, 1944–1956* (NY: Anchor, 2013), 392.

6. Hannah Arendt, *The Origins of Totalitarianism* (NY: Harcourt, 1973), 478.

7. Arendt, *Origins of Totalitarianism*, 317.

8. Yascha Mounk (@Yascha_Mounk), "It's telling that, in the year of 2019, the notion that one purpose of civics education might be to . . ." Twitter, September 13, 2019, 10:59 a.m., twitter.com/Yascha_Mounk/status/1172540349622800384.

9. Arendt, *Origins of Totalitarianism*, 330.

10. Arendt, *Origins of Totalitarianism*, 332.

11. James H. Billington, *The Icon and the Axe: An Interpretive History of Russian Culture* (NY: Vintage, 1970), 492.

12. Billington, *Icon and the Axe*, 502.

13. Heda Margolius Kovály, *Under a Cruel Star: A Life in Prague 1941–1968* (Lexington, MA: Plunkett Lake Press, 2010), loc. 11 of 201, Kindle.

14. Arendt, *Origins of Totalitarianism*, 333.

15. Jake Silverstein, "Why We Published the 1619 Project," *New York Times*, December 20, 2019, nytimes.com/interactive/2019/12/20/magazine/1619-intro.html.

16. Jeff Barrus, "Nikole Hannah-Jones Wins Pulitzer Prize for 1619 Project," Pulitzer Center, May 4, 2019, pulitzercenter.org/blog/nikole-hannah-jones-wins-pulitzer-prize-1619-project.

17. Arendt, *Origins of Totalitarianism*, 353.

18. Zack Goldberg (@zachg932), "1/n Spent some time on LexisNexis over the weekend. Depending on your political orientation, what follows will either disturb or encourage you. . . ." Twitter, May 28, 2019, 1:32 p.m., twitter.com/zachg932/status/1133440945201061888.

19. Arendt, *Origins of Totalitarianism*, 351.

20. N. V. Krylenko, "The Party Crushed," in *The Great Terror: A Reassessment*, ed. Robert Conquest (NY: Oxford University Press, 1990), 249.

21. Arendt, *Origins of Totalitarianism,* 339.
22. Michael Kruse, "I Need Loyalty," *Politico,* March 3, 2018, politico.com/magazine/story/2018/03/06/donald-trump-loyalty-staff-217227.
23. James Davison Hunter, *To Change the World: The Irony, Tragedy, and Possibility of Christianity in the Late Modern World* (NY: Oxford University Press, 2010), 38.
24. Hunter, *Change the World,* 41.
25. Czesław Miłosz, *The Captive Mind* (NY: Vintage, 1990), 3.
26. Silvester Krčméry, MD, *This Saved Us: How to Survive Brainwashing* (self-pub., 1996), 222.
27. Arendt, *Origins of Totalitarianism,* 440.

CHAPTER THREE: PROGRESSIVISM AS RELIGION

1. Milan Kundera, *The Book of Laughter and Forgetting,* trans. Michael Henry Heim (NY: Viking, 1987), 179.
2. James H. Billington, *The Icon and the Axe: An Interpretive History of Russian Culture* (NY: Vintage, 1970), 504.
3. Milan Kundera, *The Unbearable Lightness of Being,* trans. Michael Henry Heim (NY: Harper & Row, 1984), 257.
4. Yuri Slezkine, *The House of Government: A Saga of the Russian Revolution* (Princeton, NJ: Princeton University Press, 2019), 107.
5. President George W. Bush, "Bush: No Justice without Freedom," CNN, January 20, 2005, cnn.com/2005/ALLPOLITICS/01/20/bush.transcript/index.html.
6. John Gray, *Gray's Anatomy: Selected Writings* (London: Allen Lane, 2009), 273.
7. Slezkine, *House of Government,* 54.

8. Martin Latsis, quoted in Anna Geifman, *Death Orders: The Vanguard of Modern Terrorism in Revolutionary Russia* (Santa Barbara, CA: Praeger, 2010), 126.
9. James A. Lindsay and Mike Nayna, "Postmodern Religion and the Faith of Social Justice," *Areo*, December 18, 2018, areomagazine.com/2018/12/18/postmodern-religion-and-the-faith-of-social-justice/.
10. Michael Hanby, "The Brave New World of Same-Sex Marriage," *The Federalist*, February 19, 2014, thefederalist.com/2014/02/19/the-brave-new-world-of-same-sex-marriage/.
11. Pope John Paul II, *Dominum et Vivificantem*, May 18, 1986, para. 38.

CHAPTER FOUR: CAPITALISM, WOKE AND WATCHFUL

1. Parag Khanna, "These 25 Companies Are More Powerful Than Many Countries," *Foreign Policy*, March 3, 2016, foreignpolicy.com/2016/03/15/these-25-companies-are-more-powerful-than-many-countries-multinational-corporate-wealth-power/.
2. Heather Mac Donald, *The Diversity Delusion: How Race and Gender Pandering Corrupt the University and Undermine Our Culture* (NY: St. Martin's Press, 2018), 30.
3. Larry Fink, "A Sense of Purpose," BlackRock, 2018, blackrock.com/corporate/investor-relations/2018-larry-fink-ceo-letter.
4. Sarah Perez, "Over a Quarter of US Adults Now Own a Smart Speaker, Typically an Amazon Echo," Tech Crunch, March 8, 2019, techcrunch.com/2019/03/08/over-a-quarter-of-u-s-adults-now-own-a-smart-speaker-typically-an-amazon-echo/.

5. Shoshana Zuboff, quoted in "'The Goal Is to Automate Us': Welcome to the Age of Surveillance Capitalism," *The Guardian*, January 20, 2019, theguardian.com/technology/2019 /jan/20/shoshana-zuboff-age-of-surveillance-capitalism -google-facebook.

6. Caleb Parke, "Conservatives Call for PayPal Boycott After CEO Says Southern Poverty Law Center Helps Ban Users," Fox News, February 28, 2019, foxnews.com/tech/conservatives -call-for-paypal-boycott-after-ceo-admits-splc-helps-ban-users.

7. Michelle Malkin, "Is This Bank Chasing Away Conservatives?," *National Review*, April 15, 2019, nationalreview.com /2019/04/chase-bank-conservative-customers/.

8. Katanga Johnson, "U.S. Gun Lobby Takes Aim at 'Gun-Hating' Banks Citi, BofA," Reuters, May 18, 2018, reuters .com/article/us-usa-guns-banks/u-s-gun-lobby-takes-aim-at -gun-hating-banks-citi-bofa-idUSKCN1IJ260.

9. Shoshana Zuboff, *The Age of Surveillance Capitalism: The Fight for a Human Future at the New Frontier of Power* (NY: Public Affairs, 2019), loc. 5421, Kindle.

10. Douglas Murray, *The Madness of Crowds: Gender, Race and Identity* (NY: Bloomsbury Continuum, 2019), loc. 2155, Kindle.

11. Edward Snowden, *Permanent Record* (NY: Metropolitan Books, 2019), 178.

12. Matt Sledge, "CIA's Gus Hunt on Big Data: We 'Try to Collect Everything and Hang On to It Forever," *Huffington Post*, March 20, 2013, huffingtonpost.com.au/entry/cia-gus-hunt -big-data_n_2917842.

13. Editorial, "How China Corralled 1 Million Uighurs into Concentration Camps," *Washington Post*, February 29, 2020, washingtonpost.com/opinions/global-opinions/a

-spreadsheet-of-those-in-hell-how-china-corralled-uighurs
-into-concentration-camps/2020/02/28/4daeca4a-58c8
-11ea-ab68-101ecfec2532_story.html.

14. John Lanchester, "Document Number Nine," *London Review of Books*, October 10, 2019, lrb.co.uk/the-paper/v41/n19/john -lanchester/document-number-nine.

15. Kai Strittmatter, *We Have Been Harmonized: Life in China's Surveillance State*, trans. Ruth Martin (London: Old Street Publishing, 2019), loc. 1213, Kindle.

16. Strittmatter, *Surveillance*, loc. 1224, Kindle.

17. Milan Kundera, *The Unbearable Lightness of Being*, trans. Michael Henry Heim (NY: Harper & Row, 1984), 112–13.

18. Jean Twenge, "Have Smartphones Destroyed a Generation?," *The Atlantic*, September 2017, theatlantic.com/magazine /archive/2017/09/has-the-smartphone-destroyed-a -generation/534198/.

CHAPTER FIVE: VALUE NOTHING MORE THAN TRUTH

1. Václav Havel, *The Power of the Powerless: Citizens Against the State in Central-Eastern Europe*, trans. Paul Wilson (Armonk, NY: M. E. Sharpe, 1992), 39.

2. Havel, *Powerless*, 39–40.

3. Havel, *Powerless*, 45.

CHAPTER SIX: CULTIVATE CULTURAL MEMORY

1. Victims of Communism Memorial Foundation, *Annual Report on US Attitudes toward Socialism, Communism, and Collectivism* (Washington, DC: 2019), victimsofcommunism.org/2019 -annual-poll.

2. Laura M. Nicolae, "100 Years. 100 Million Lives. Think Twice," *Harvard Crimson*, November 20, 2017, thecrimson.com /article/2017/11/20/nicolae-one-hundred-million/.

3. Milan Kundera, *The Book of Laughter and Forgetting*, trans. Michael Henry Heim (NY: Viking, 1987), 187.

4. Paul Connerton, *How Societies Remember* (Cambridge: Cambridge University Press, 1989), 3.

5. Leszek Kołakowski, *Is God Happy? Selected Essays* (NY: Penguin Classics, 2012), 60.

6. Cardinal Joseph Ratzinger, "Homily Pro Eligendo Romano Pontifice," April 18, 2005, vatican.va/gpII/documents/homily -pro-eligendo-pontifice_20050418_en.html.

7. Connerton, *Societies Remember*, 73

8. Oliver Bullough, *The Last Man in Russia: The Struggle to Save a Dying Nation* (NY: Basic Books, 2013), 42, or loc. 788 of 5895, Kindle.

9. Václav Benda, *The Long Night of the Watchman: Essays by Václav Benda, 1977–1989*, ed. F. Flagg Taylor IV, trans. Barbara Day (South Bend, IN: St. Augustine's Press, 2017), 218.

10. Roger Scruton, *Notes from Underground* (NY: Beaufort Books, 2014), 54–55, or loc. 760 of 3188, Kindle.

CHAPTER SEVEN: FAMILIES ARE RESISTANCE CELLS

1. Václav Benda, *The Long Night of the Watchman: Essays by Václav Benda, 1977–1989*, ed. F. Flagg Taylor IV, trans. Barbara Day (South Bend, IN: St. Augustine's Press, 2017), 222–32.

2. Benda, *Watchman*, 225.

3. Benda, *Watchman*, 225–26.
4. Benda, *Watchman*, 226.
5. Benda, *Watchman*, 228.

CHAPTER EIGHT: RELIGION, THE BEDROCK OF RESISTANCE

1. Silvester Krčméry, MD, *This Saved Us: How to Survive Brainwashing* (self-pub., 1996), 81.
2. Krčméry, *This Saved Us*, 100.
3. Bullough, *The Last Man in Russia*, 85 or loc. 1594 of 5895, Kindle.
4. George Calciu, *Interviews, Homilies, and Talks* (Platina, CA: St. Herman of Alaska Brotherhood, 2010), 187.

CHAPTER NINE: STANDING IN SOLIDARITY

1. Aleksandr Solzhenitsyn, *The Gulag Archipelago 1918–1956*, trans. Thomas P. Whitney and Harry Willetts; abr. by Edward E. Ericson Jr. (NY: Perennial, 1983), 86.

CHAPTER TEN: THE GIFT OF SUFFERING

1. Carrie Dann, "'A Deep and Boiling Anger': NBC/WSJ Poll Finds a Pessimistic America Despite Current Economic Satisfaction," NBC News, August 25, 2019, nbcnews.com/politics/meet-the-press/deep-boiling-anger-nbc-wsj-poll-finds-pessimistic-america-despite-n1045916.
2. Søren Kierkegaard, *Provocations: Spiritual Writings of Kierkegaard* (Farmington, PA: Plough Publishing, 1999), 85.

3. Kierkegaard, *Provocations*, 88.
4. Silvester Krčméry, MD, *This Saved Us: How to Survive Brainwashing* (self-pub., 1996), 56.
5. Krčméry, *This Saved Us*, 163.
6. Aleksandr Solzhenitsyn, *The Gulag Archipelago 1918–1956*, trans. Thomas P. Whitney and Harry Willetts; abr. by Edward E. Ericson Jr. (NY: Perennial, 1983), 313.
7. "Testimony of Rev. Richard Wurmbrand before the US Senate (1966): Communist Exploitation of Religion," May 6, 1966, Joseph Smith Foundation, josephsmithfoundation.org /testimony-of-rev-richard-wurmbrand-before-the-u-s-senate -1966-communist-exploitation-of-religion/.
8. Wurmbrand, US Senate.
9. Richard Wurmbrand, *The Midnight Bride* (Bartlesville, OK: Living Sacrifice, 2009), loc. 713 of 3025, Kindle.
10. George Calciu, *Interviews, Homilies, and Talks* (Platina, CA: St. Herman of Alaska Brotherhood, 2010), 109.
11. Calciu, *Interviews*, 110.
12. Calciu, *Interviews*, 111.
13. Calciu, *Interviews*, 112.
14. Calciu, *Interviews*, 131.
15. Richard Wurmbrand, *In God's Underground* (Bartlesville, OK: Living Sacrifice, 2004), loc. 661, Kindle.

CONCLUSION: LIVE NOT BY LIES

1. Aldous Huxley, *Brave New World*, Huxley, accessed May 18, 2020, huxley.net/bnw/seventeen.html.

2. Lubomir Gleiman, *From the Maelstrom: A Pilgrim's Story of Dissent and Survival in the Twentieth Century* (Bloomington, IN: Author House, 2011), 103.

3. Aleksandr Solzhenitsyn, "Live Not by Lies!," in Orthodoxy Today, accessed June 2, 2020, orthodoxytoday.org/articles/SolhenitsynLies.php.

INDEX

INDEX

INDEX

INDEX

INDEX

239